IMAGES
of America

OREGON SHAKESPEARE
FESTIVAL

Founder Angus L. Bowmer is pictured on the Oregon Shakespeare Festival (OSF) campus in 1974. "The great secret Angus had, and which he shared with his public," noted producing director Jerry Turner, "was that a theater deals with human commonplaces accessible to us all. In the works of Shakespeare and . . . all the great playwrights, there are human truths that need expression so we can all know, most vividly, what it is to be alive." (Courtesy of the OSF Archives.)

ON THE COVER: The 2005 production of *Love's Labor's Lost*, directed by Kenneth Albers, featured the scenic design of Marjorie Bradley Kellogg, costumes by Susan E. Mickey, and lighting by Robert Peterson. The actors onstage are, from left to right, Brent Harris, Jeff Cummings, Christopher DuVal, and Jose Luis Sanchez. (Courtesy of T. Charles Erickson.)

IMAGES
of America

OREGON SHAKESPEARE
FESTIVAL

To Nancy –
Thanks for your help with
this. Enjoy! KFL
& Amy

Kathleen F. Leary and Amy E. Richard
Oregon Shakespeare Festival

ARCADIA
PUBLISHING

ACKNOWLEDGMENTS

There are many people to thank in the building of this book, but in particular Angus Bowmer and Bill Patton for being champion pack rats, which allowed us to verify a multitude of myths and faulty memories with primary sources of factual information found within the OSF archives. Without the formation of the archives, set in motion by Kay Atwood's research for the Design and Exhibit Center 35 years ago, the task would have been much more difficult.

For the information about Ashland's early years, the sources were Marjorie O'Harra's *Ashland: the First 130 Years*; V. William Oyler Jr.'s doctoral dissertation, *The Festival Story: A History of the Oregon Shakespearean Festival*; and Megan E. Geigner's thesis for Reed College, *The Southern Oregon Chautauqua Association: Building the Foundation of the Oregon Shakespeare Festival*. Thanks to the Southern Oregon Historical Society for photographs, and Terry Skibby, who along with many photographs, provided clarifying historical details.

Angus Bowmer's autobiography, *As I remember, Adam*, supplied a wealth of information, and we thank all the writers of the festival's past publications—souvenir programs, newsletters, prologues, and brochures, which were an invaluable source of information. We also thank those who took time to share their memories of their work here: Bill and Shirley Patton, Richard Hay, Pat Patton, Kathy Oyler, Judy Bjorlie, Judy Kennedy, Nora Yeoman, and others.

Kudos to the volunteers in the festival archives, Judy Kennedy, Nancy Menken, and Barbara Seropian, who pulled the photographs and who will undoubtedly refile them. Huge thanks to Jenny Graham, staff photographer, who scanned and prepared all the photographs, and to the photographers: Rick Adams, Christopher Briscoe, David Cooper, T. Charles Erickson, Jenny Graham, Andrée Lanthier, Hank Kranzler, Jennifer Reiley, and others.

We appreciate those who read through this and made valuable suggestions: Kimberley Jean Barry, Nan Christensen, Catherine Foster, Paul Nicholson, Bill Rauch, and Hilary Tate. And thanks to Linda Fern, Mallory Pierce, Ed Pearson, and Fritz Schneider for additional support. Finally thank you to Sarah Higginbotham at Arcadia Publishing, who approached us about this book.

Unless otherwise noted, all images appearing are courtesy of the OSF archives.

INTRODUCTION

Through the years, journalists, city officials, scholars, and students from across the country have visited the Oregon Shakespeare Festival to puzzle out how a nationally renowned theater came to be located in a rural town of southwest Oregon. Ashland is 350 miles from Oregon's largest city and seems an unlikely locale for a professional theater with a budget of $24 million. The theater operates in rotating repertory on three stages and produces 11 shows with more than 780 performances, and has one of the largest theater education programs in the world.

The festival's founder, Angus L. Bowmer, reflecting in later years on the growth of the organization—and undoubtedly on the vast number of queries as to how he had achieved such success—said, "Theatre must come from the people. You cannot superimpose theatre on a local culture." Henry Woronicz, the festival's third artistic director, noted, "It has always been Ashland, the place that allowed the work to spring to life, and it is Ashland that will fashion the possibilities yet to come."

Ashland is a different community from what it was when Bowmer produced the First Annual Shakespearean Festival in 1935 during the city's Fourth of July celebration. In size and spirit, however, Ashland remains a small town, and its early motto, "Industry, Education, Temperance—Ashland Honors Those Who Foster These," has not been completely erased from its consciousness. That early commitment to industry and education (temperance was not so fully embraced; by the 1880s, Ashland had five saloons) shaped a community that provided the essential elements for the eventual birth of an annual Shakespearean festival.

The first emigrants to Ashland settled in 1852. Residents started the first school in 1854 and in 1872, facilitated the opening of an institution of higher learning. Financial difficulties and numerous closures plagued the Normal School, as it came to be known, but finally, urged by Ashland residents, the state legislature in 1926 appropriated funds to reestablish what is now Southern Oregon University.

Ashland thrived in the early years, and by 1874, when the town incorporated, its population was 300. Ten years later, the first train from the north whistled into Ashland, the southern terminus of Southern Pacific's Portland line. On December 17, 1887, the golden spike was driven in at Ashland's railroad yard, connecting the northern line with Southern Pacific's San Francisco line and making it possible to bring in new residents and travelers.

Ashlanders of the time held education, culture, and the arts dear to their hearts. The *Ashland Daily Tidings*, first published in 1876, printed the news. The Ganiard Opera House provided a venue for plays and music, as well as basketball games and high school graduations. The Ashland Brass Band was organized in 1890 and performed at community events and Fourth of July celebrations. Ladies of the community formed the Ashland Library Association, keeping an eye toward establishing a building to house the growing collection.

In the 1880s and 1890s, an adult educational movement called Chautauqua gained popularity across the country, bringing entertainers, teachers, musicians, preachers, orators, and other specialists to rural areas. In 1892, residents formed the Southern Oregon Chautauqua Association. After some debate, it was agreed that Ashland, with its electric lights, city water, and good hotels, would be the best site in the valley.

The decision was fortuitous for the community and its future. The first Chautauqua hall opened in 1893 and could accommodate 1,000 people. The event was so popular that the dome was enlarged in 1905 to accommodate 1,500 people, and again in 1917 to seat 5,000. Among those who presented at the Ashland Chautauqua were John Phillip Sousa's band, the preacher Billy Sunday, and the orator William Jennings Bryan. The Chautauqua grounds were improved and acreage was gradually added, becoming the first park in southern Oregon and later named Lithia Park.

By the 1920s, Chautauqua's prominence was fading. Radio, movie houses, automobiles, and other venues (Medford's new Craterian Theater and Ashland's Lithia Theatre) offered people a variety of opportunities for entertainment. The community hated to see the Chautauqua building demolished, however, so residents passed a bond to purchase the dome and grounds and add them to Lithia Park. Despite this commitment, by 1933, the dome was so deteriorated that Works Progress Administration (WPA) workers tore it down, leaving only the circular perimeter wall and a rudimentary stage.

A few years earlier, in 1931, Bowmer arrived in town to instruct English at the Southern Oregon Normal School. A man passionate about drama, and in particular Shakespeare performed on an Elizabethan stage, he was terribly disappointed to learn that the Normal School had no theater program.

Imagine his wonder when in 1933, hunkered near the old Chautauqua stage to avoid a driving March rain, he noticed that the circle of roofless concrete walls bore a peculiar resemblance to 17th-century sketches of Shakespeare's Globe Theatre. "This comparison," he noted in his autobiography *When I remember, Adam*, "stimulated the germinal idea of a Shakespearean festival."

Supported by friends, students, and colleagues, Bowmer produced the First Annual Oregon Shakespearean Festival July 2–4, 1935, with two performances of *Twelfth Night* and one performance of *The Merchant of Venice*. The festival continued the next five years, but closed during World War II. In 1947, the Ashland Chamber of Commerce urged Bowmer to revive the festival. He decided that for $1,000 he would, reasoning that if the festival were to survive, Ashland must want the festival very much and that "we theater people should be essential to the success of the community's artistic project."

From 1935 through 1969, the festival almost exclusively produced Shakespeare. Attendance skyrocketed in the 1960s, and record numbers of people were turned away. With limited capacity for seating and revenue, it became necessary to build a new theater. With the opening of the Angus Bowmer Theatre in 1970, the season expanded into the spring and fall, and new repertory was developed, adding Western classics to the playbill. In 1977, a small black box space, the Black Swan, was designed in an existing building on Pioneer Street. The space provided an opportunity for the company to present old and new plays that were not performed frequently, as they were deemed risky or unpopular. Eventually the Black Swan was consistently at more than 95 percent of capacity, so in 2002, the state-of-the-art New Theatre opened.

The festival's history has always been one of invention and continuity. In the past 75 years, Bowmer and four successive artistic directors, Jerry Turner, Henry Woronicz, Libby Appel, and Bill Rauch, and only two full-time executive directors since 1950, William Patton and Paul Nicholson, have steered the organization. Recognizing the inevitability of change, each has sought to preserve the best of the past and promote change in response to need and artistic endeavor. Angus Bowmer understood that "the economic value of art, no matter how great, is short-lived unless the aesthetic values are the result of skill and integrity." Supported through the decades by staff, volunteers, members, the Rogue Valley business community, and the City of Ashland, the Oregon Shakespeare Festival continues to produce that transformative art.

One

SETTING THE STAGE
1893–1934

In his autobiography *As I remember, Adam*, Angus Bowmer wrote about the important role of accident, coincidence, and fate in the development of the Oregon Shakespeare Festival. Years before the festival was founded, however, it seems that fate played a title role in preparing Ashland and Bowmer for their meeting in 1931.

In Chautauqua, New York, in 1874, decades before Bowmer was born, a nationwide movement was founded, spreading arts and culture across the country. The residents of Ashland, eager to capitalize on this educational opportunity, supported the building of an independent Chautauqua dome in 1893.

While Ashland was enjoying the benefits of the Chautauqua summer camps, Bowmer's grandmother was drilling him for declamatory contests in Oak Harbor, Washington. She also taught him that society rewards people for service to society. Bowmer reports that at age nine, he felt he would do something important, but as he felt himself to be the least talented in his family, he decided to specialize in something that no one else would. Because no one else was doing it, he would become the best in his family. Little did he realize that his specialty would be the performance of Shakespeare on an Elizabethan stage.

Years later as a theater student at the University of Washington, Bowmer met B. Iden Payne, a theater scholar and director, who inspired Bowmer's love for Shakespearean production on an Elizabethan stage. Upon graduation, Bowmer sought a position teaching drama and speech, and in 1931, in the midst of the Depression, he was fortunate to find a position training grade school teachers at Southern Oregon Normal School.

Though there was no drama department, Bowmer found ways to satisfy his theatrical creativity and to discover potential audiences as well as people key to his future theater. And always there was the roofless Chautauqua structure and its likeness to Shakespeare's Old Globe that excited Bowmer's imagination. Here he and his friends hoped to build a Shakespearean festival and revive the tradition of Chautauqua's summer festival.

Ashland of the 1880s and 1890s was a town of roughly 900 residents. The railway provided north-south travel, and stagecoach lines took goods and passengers over the Siskiyou Mountains and Greensprings. The Ashland Electric Power and Light Company generated enough electricity to light the city's streets and homes. Left of center is the first Chautauqua dome, built in 1893. The Southern Oregon Chautauqua Association (SOCA) was formed in 1892 by Rev. J. S. Smith, who had suggested the series be held in Central Point. Reverend Stratton of Portland University argued that Ashland was a better site, with more amenities and a lovely campsite in Roper's Grove on the banks of Ashland Creek. Among the amenities were the Ashland Hotel (large building, center) and the Ganiard Opera House (to the right of the hotel). (Courtesy of Terry Skibby Collection.)

The Chautauqua dome in Ashland was erected in 1893 in 10 days; the first performance was held on July 5. The program ran from the 5th through the 14th and cost $1 for the entire 10 days. The dome was 80 feet high and 40 feet wide, without interior posts or pillars. The inside had a dirt floor, canvas window coverings, and could accommodate 1,000 people. The acoustics were said to be excellent. Located above the downtown plaza, it was called the Chautauqua Tabernacle. SOCA paid for the building and talent by selling $10 bonds to local businesses and individuals. In 1894, G. F. Billings was elected president of SOCA.

The Grand Army of the Republic (GAR) building, pictured here in the early 1900s, was constructed for activities for veterans of the Union army who had served in the Civil War. The building, later referred to as Pioneer Hall, became the YMCA and was located along the Chautauqua walkway and adjacent to the Chautauqua grounds. (Courtesy of Terry Skibby Collection.)

The Ashland City Band has its roots in the Ashland Brass Band, formed in the 1880s. Under the able guidance of Otis Helman, appointed director in 1890, the brass band became widely known and was sought after for parties and dances. The band gave regular concerts on the Chautauqua grounds under a small gazebo, and it played each year in the Fourth of July parade. (Courtesy of Terry Skibby Collection.)

The Chautauqua series experienced such popularity that the 1893 dome soon became inadequate to support expanding audiences. In 1905, SOCA enlarged the building by cutting it in half, moving half up the hill, and filling the gap to create an oblong building. The new space accommodated 1,500 people. The tower adjacent to the Chautauqua building was a water tower used by the fire department. (Courtesy of Terry Skibby Collection.)

Members of SOCA pose with guest speaker William Jennings Bryan and his wife, Mary (with flowers, center), at a reception on the Chautauqua grounds in Ashland on January 25, 1907. In 1982, OSF produced the play *Inherit the Wind*, in which one of the main characters is modeled on Bryan, the famous orator. (Courtesy of Southern Oregon Historical Society, negative 6748)

Ever-increasing Chautauqua audiences led SOCA president G. F. Billings and others to suggest that a new amphitheater be constructed. The building was enlarged a third time in 1917 at a cost of $15,000, largely financed by a city bond. The new building included a 14-foot reinforced concrete wall, dressing rooms, and a ticket booth. The local paper reported that 20 carpenters installed 126 ribs in the roof, each 180 feet in length. The roof was 160 feet at its greatest width, 180 feet in length, and 60 feet high at the center. The dome had a seating capacity of 5,000, and the stage could accommodate 700 people. (Courtesy of Terry Skibby Collection.)

The Chautauqua grounds (c. 1925) expanded in December 1908 when Ashland residents voted to dedicate the old mill site on the plaza and all city-owned property bordering Ashland Creek up the forest reserve as a city park. In 1913, the park board purchased 45 acres of land south of the grounds along the creek, providing additional campgrounds for Chautauqua. (Courtesy of Terry Skibby Collection.)

The Ladies' Chautauqua Park Club was organized to improve the Chautauqua grounds. The women raised enough money through community events to plant lawns, trees, and flower beds and hire a gardener. To the left of the GAR canon is a gazebo where the Ashland Brass Band played for certain occasions. The city hall tower can be seen behind the structure. (Courtesy of Terry Skibby Collection.)

Many Chautauqua participants camped in the tents along the creek in Roper's Grove. By 1897, SOCA was renting tents to campers for $1.50 for the season, and season ticket holders were able to camp for free in the grove. The Ladies' Chautauqua Park Club made certain the grounds were improved before each annual session began. (Courtesy of Terry Skibby Collection.)

In addition to Chautauqua and the park, Ashland's mineral springs and sulfur baths drew numerous visitors. The Natatorium was built in 1909, and included two pools and a dance floor. In the 1930s, the cover was torn off, but the pools were kept and renamed the Twin Plunges. Those pools were demolished in the 1970s. (Courtesy of Terry Skibby Collection.)

Angus Bowmer played the role of teddy bear in his first-ever performance in a variety show at the Sumas, Washington, Methodist church (c. 1910). The show was billed the *Teddy Bear Picnic*, and Angus "did a ludicrous dance costumed as a teddy bear," according to his father. The young Angus Bowmer is seated first row, center.

Angus Bowmer's paternal grandparents, along with his parents, instilled in him a dedication to public service. His grandfather Harry started 16 newspapers in the Pacific Northwest. Due to their nomadic lifestyle, the grandparents lived in tents. Grandmother Minnie Bowmer drilled Angus in declamation, teaching that the expression of any idea must start with the diaphragm. Bowmer felt her teaching had begun his preparation for the Elizabethan stage.

In 1890, Oscar and Lucinda Ganiard built the Ganiard Opera House on the corner of Pioneer and Main Streets. It was said to be the finest hall between San Francisco and Portland. The upstairs stage seated 800 and was used for basketball games, dramatic presentations, and graduations. The building burned in 1912, but the first floor and basement were salvaged and are still in use today. (Courtesy of Terry Skibby Collection.)

Photographer F. L. Camps started his business in a wooden building that was replaced in 1904 by a brick structure that currently houses OSF offices and the Chauteaulin Restaurant, to the left of the Chautauqua walkway. OSF's costume shop now occupies the second floor of the Pioneer Building, to the right of the walkway. (Courtesy of Terry Skibby Collection.)

The First National Bank opened in 1910, and the grand clock helped add to the building's reputation as one of the most modern to date. Located on the corner of Pioneer and Main Streets, the clock continues to tell time, and the building now houses OSF's administrative offices. The bank vault remains a storage area. (Courtesy of Southern Oregon Historical Society, negative 6512.)

Fortmillers' Department Store (now Earthly Goods) was built on East Main Street in 1925. The First Church of Christ, Scientist, located up Pioneer Street across from the Chautauqua dome, was constructed in 1923. The building was purchased by OSF in 1973 and named Carpenter Hall after the Carpenter family, a prominent family in the valley that was extremely supportive of the festival. (Courtesy of Terry Skibby Collection.)

Angus Bowmer, in his first Shakespearean role, played Adam in *As You Like It* at Bellingham Normal School's production in the late 1920s. The show was staged on a wooded knoll on the school's campus. Bowmer is seated at the far left. His instructor in Expression, Victor H. Hoppe, is standing second from left. Professor Hoppe directed the show and played Jaques.

This production of *Love's Labour's Lost* was directed by Angus Bowmer's mentor, B. Iden Payne, at the University of Washington in 1930. John Conway, acting head of the theater department, embellished the stage to resemble an Elizabethan theater. Bowmer, in the enormous ruff, played Boyet. While working with Payne, Bowmer was first inspired by the idea of Shakespeare produced on an Elizabethan stage.

Due to funding issues, Southern Oregon Normal School had closed its doors in 1909, but the community continued to push for the establishment of a state college. By 1925, state legislators responded. The building pictured was constructed on land purchased by the city, and doors opened in June 1926. J. A. Churchill was elected president of the college, and the building was later named after him. (Courtesy of Terry Skibby Collection.)

Angus Bowmer's first production of Shakespeare—a modern dress, no-expense version of *As You Like It*—was produced at Southern Oregon Normal School. Bowmer played Jaques and staged the lean production to raise money to subsidize the production of his full-length play, *Andrew Jackson*. He would eventually submit *Andrew Jackson* as his master's thesis at the University of Washington, but not before he saw it onstage.

Angus Bowmer wrote his second full-length play, *Oyer-Un-Gon* ("Land of Plenty" in Shoshone) in 1934, a commission by Oregon governor Julius Meier to write, produce, and direct a pageant of Oregon history, celebrating 75 years of statehood. Staged at the Medford Fairgrounds, the production featured a cast of 500, complete with horses and wagons. The first performance drew 1,800 people and was the highlight of the celebration.

The Chautauqua's great dome was removed in 1933. Angus Bowmer could not help but notice that from particular points of view, the circle of roofless concrete walls that had supported the dome bore a peculiar resemblance to 17th-century sketches of Shakespeare's Globe Theatre. "This comparison," he noted in his autobiography, "stimulated the germinal idea of a Shakespearean festival."

Two

THE DREAM BEGINS
1935–1950

From the beginning, Angus Bowmer felt that though Chautauqua had been dead in Ashland for more than 10 years, the idea of a festival, particularly one housed within the walls of the old tradition, might be alive and well in the minds of Rogue Valley residents, and what better time to stage a revival than during the Fourth of July celebrations?

Ashland had a long history of these festivities, but there had been none from 1929 to 1934. Bowmer suggested to local business and professional leaders that the tradition be renewed and that the First Annual Shakespearean Festival be included. His suggestion was met with enthusiasm, and to enhance the civic celebration, the city made use of WPA funds to build an architectural facade on the old Chautauqua platform with donated materials.

The story of the boxing matches has become a festival favorite. Shortly before the celebrations, city officials approached Bowmer about staging boxing matches in the afternoon to cover losses they feared the Shakespeare festival would incur. Bowmer agreed, but much to his delight, the festival paid for both itself and the deficit from the fights. Shakespeare was an economic success from the first year.

In 1936, the previous season's plays, *The Merchant of Venice* and *Twelfth Night*, were remounted, and *Romeo and Juliet* was added. From the beginning, the festival displayed two enduring characteristics—the performance of plays in repertory and a single company of actors to accomplish it. The festival incorporated in 1937, and by 1939, the repertoire had been increased to eight performances of four plays. *The Taming of the Shrew* was taken on tour through California and to San Francisco's Golden Gate International Exhibition, and attendance had increased from 500 to 2,000 in four short years.

Fire destroyed much of the stage and the entire wardrobe in 1940, a severe loss from which the festival had not recovered when World War II erupted. When Bowmer returned in 1947 from a stint in the army, he was asked by city leaders to revive the festival, and with support from the Ashland Chamber of Commerce, a new stage was built and four plays with 16 performances were presented that season.

By 1950, actors, technicians, and students came from all corners of the country to study and work at OSF. To assist these individuals, the Shakespeare Guild of Medford worked to establish a scholarship fund.

Because the first Shakespeare festival was to be associated with the city's Fourth of July celebration, the city used a state-supported crew (funded through WPA) to build a stage and Elizabethan facade within the Chautauqua walls. Angus Bowmer sketched a rough plan for the construction manager, using the Elizabethan stage design by John Ashby Conway that he had helped to build for B. Iden Payne at the University of Washington.

Pictured here is the Southern Oregon Normal School student production of *The Merchant of Venice*, the production that Angus Bowmer revived for the First Annual Shakespearean Festival. For the production of *Twelfth Night*, Bowmer gave roles to a number of community members. Among them were Bill Eberhart, the city editor of the *Ashland Daily Tidings*, and Dorothy Pruitt, who had acted in *Oyer-Un-Gon* in 1934.

THE CITY OF ASHLAND

— PRESENTS —

The First Annual Shakespearean Festival

"TWELFTH NIGHT" Tuesday and Thursday, 8 P. M.	Under the Direction of ANGUS L. BOWMER	"MERCHANT OF VENICE" Wednesday at 8 P. M.

The Persons of the Play—

Sebastian, brother to Viola	Dolph Janes
Antonio, friend to Sebastian	Merrill Gunter
Sea Captain, friend to Viola	Jim Foster
Valentine) Attendants to	Helen Ellenberger
Curio) Duke	Beth Cummings
Orsino, duke of Illyria	Marion Frost
Sir Toby Belch, uncle to Olivia	Angus L. Bowmer
Sir Andrew Aguecheek	John Barker
Malvolio, steward to Olivia	Geo. F. Smith
Fabian) Servants to	Bill Eberhart
Feste, a clown) Olivia	Robert Stedman
Olivia, a rich countess	Dorothy Pruitt
Viola, in love with Orsino	Jeanne Daugherty
Maria, Olivia's woman	Jeanne Fabrick
Priest	Tom Palmer
Officer	Bill Cottrell

Scene: A city in Illyria and the Sea coast near it.

PRODUCTION STAFF

Costumes designed by	Lois M. Bowmer
Construction Manager	R. Berry
Wardrobe Mistresses	Maxine Gearhart, Billie Brandes
Properties	Jeanne Fabrick
Electrician	Tom Palmer
Book Holder	Noma Weaver
Make-up	Marion Ady, Angus Bowmer
Publicity	Gordon MacCracken

Music orchestrated and directed by Lawrence Hubert

ORCHESTRA PERSONNEL

Violins

Mary Roberson	Frances Aikens
Alicia Coggins	Ruth Hardy
Florence Hubert	Laverne Roberson
Leslie Kincaid	Jean Billings

Viola

Andrew Johnson	Lorraine Sparr

Cello — Phyllis Sparr

Flute — Piano — Flossie Thompson

Reeds — Rosa Franko

The Persons of the Play—

Duke of Venice	Marion Frost
Prince of Morocco) Suitors to	John Harr
Prince of Arragon) Portia	Karl Moore
Antonio, a Merchant of Venice	Ed. Butze
Bassanio, his friend	Robert Stedman
Gratiano) Friends to	Geo. F. Smith
Salanio) Antonio and	Merrill Gunter
Salarino) Bassanio	Tom Palmer
Lorenzo, in love with Jessica	Jim Foster
Shylock, a rich Jew	Angus L. Bowmer
Launcelot Gobbo	John Chipley
	A servant to Shylock
Old Gobbo, father to Launcelot	Bill Cottrell
Leonardo, servant to Bassanio	Helen Ellenberger
Stephano, servant to Portia	Beth Cummings
Tubal, friend to Shylock	Bill Cottrell
Portia, a rich heiress	Helen Edmiston
Nerissa, her waiting maid	Beverly Young
Jessica, daughter to Shylock	Wanada Aldrich
Curtain boys	Audrey Lofland, Wilma Copple
Magnificoes and other attendants:	Bob Root, Maxine Gearhart, Vernon Clark, Jack Sanderson, Don Darnielle.

Scene: Partly at Venice and partly at Belmont, the seat of Portia, on the continent.

Preparation for the First Annual Shakespearean Festival was intense. Normal School students and faculty were in class during the mornings, and rehearsals, construction, and technical work occurred during afternoons and evenings. Throwaway programs were created for the first two years of the festival; a souvenir program was created in the third. As Angus Bowmer noted, the word *annual* was proof that he and his friends had permanency in mind.

As the Fourth of July drew near, the celebration committee, believing the plays would result in a deficit to the city budget, proposed that boxing matches be held on the Elizabethan Stage. Angus Bowmer agreed, and 42 rounds were held in the afternoon. To his great pleasure, the plays not only paid for themselves but also for the deficit in the boxing matches, proving that Shakespeare could be an economic asset.

Twelfth Night played on July 2 and 4, and *The Merchant of Venice* on July 3. Jeanne Daugherty and George F. Smith played Viola and Malvolio in *Twelfth Night*. The plays were directed by Angus Bowmer, and costumes were designed by Lois M. Bowmer, Bowmer's first wife. Others in the cast, who would become key players in the development of the festival, included Robert Stedman and William Cottrell.

Angus Bowmer played Shylock in the 1935 production of *The Merchant of Venice* and in seven subsequent productions. He noted that his early Shylocks were simply bad men, but he later realized that Shylock needed to be a human that people could recognize. "He might be stingy, he might be funny, but he still feels pain and is capable of being destroyed by the people around him who do not understand him."

Angus Bowmer also played Sir Toby Belch in the 1935 festival. The following year, Bowmer remounted *The Merchant of Venice* and *Twelfth Night* and added a third production, *Romeo and Juliet*. He not only directed all three productions, but he again played Shylock and Sir Toby plus the roles of Mercutio and Friar John.

Angus Bowmer and Lois Muzzall were married September 11, 1926. They attended Bellingham Normal School in Washington and taught grade school in a number of towns in the state of Washington. Lois was art director at the festival from 1935 to 1940 and created both costumes and scenery. She and Angus divorced in May 1940. Lois moved to Southern California to pursue her art after the 1940 season.

Dorothy Pruitt (left) and Doreen Leverette pose with a gas station attendant during a 1938 publicity tour through Oregon. Festival members traveled to Salem to talk with Gov. Charles H. Martin, who had attended the festival in the 1937 season. They presented the governor with an honorary membership, and on their return trip stopped in various cities to speak with newspaper editors and writers.

The 1939 Golden Gate International Exposition in San Francisco presented a golden opportunity for a national publicity campaign for Ashland and the festival. Using a city grant of $500 and $500 borrowed against Angus Bowmer's own insurance policy, plus money raised from a benefit performance, the festival traveled south. The 40 actors participating dressed in Elizabethan outfits made for street wear the entire three days in the city.

OSF actors performed *The Taming of the Shrew* at the Golden Gate International Exposition, but the main event was a live national broadcast on NBC radio of an hour-long adaptation of *Shrew*. Panic ensued when actors discovered shortly before broadcast that the 17 scripts were missing. After fruitless searching, Dorothy Pruitt remembered that NBC had one advance script. Sixteen typists stepped forward, and scripts were rushed to the actors as they read.

Page 34

PETRUCHIO

Marry, peace it bodes, and love and quiet life,
And awful rule and right supremacy; and to be
Short, what not that's sweet and happy ?

BAPTISTA

Now fair befall thee, good Petruchio!
The wager thou hast won; and I will add unto
Their losses twenty thousand crowns,
Another dowry to another daughter,
For she is changed as she had never been.

PETRUCHIO

Nay, I will win my wager better yet///
See where she comes and brings your froward wives
As prisoners to her womanly persuasion...
Katherina, that cap of yours becomes you not!
Off with that bauble and throw it under foot.

WIDOW

Lord, let me never have a cause to sigh,
Till I be brought to such a silly pass.

BIANCA

Fie! What a foolish duty call you this?

LUCENTIO

I would your duty were as foolish too!
The wisdom of your duty, fair Bianca,
Hath cost me an hundred crowns since supper time.

BIANCA

The more fool you, for laying on my duty.

PETRUCHIO

Katherine, I charge thee, tell these headstrong
Women what duty they do owe their lords and husbands.

WIDOW

Come, come, you're mocking; we will have no telling.

PETRUCHIO

Come on, I say; and first begin with her.

WIDOW

She shall not.

The festival has a long history of participation in Ashland's Fourth of July parade. In this 1939 photograph, Lillian Davis of Klamath Falls, Oregon, plays the official Queen Elizabeth in the parade. A queen was selected to act as a goodwill ambassador for the festival for intermittent seasons until 1955.

The ruler over the 1940 festival was 19-year-old queen Mary Shreve of Medford, Oregon. She and her three southern Oregon princesses, Phyllis Collier, Marylynn Sherlock, and Carol McCollum, invited Gov. Charles A. Sprague to attend the festival during a goodwill trip through Oregon. This was the first year attendants were selected to accompany the queen on her tours.

Angus Bowmer took a leave of absence from OSF in 1940, a year before it went dark for six years. He married Gertrude Butler in 1940 and two years later entered the army as a supply sergeant at Fort Jackson, South Carolina. He transferred to Douglas Aircraft Company in Santa Monica, and during that time he met Bing Crosby, who was an honorary director of the festival from 1949 to 1951.

In 1947, Angus Bowmer accepted an invitation from the Ashland Chamber of Commerce to restart the festival, once it was agreed that he would be paid $1,000. The stage, which had been heavily damaged in a 1940 fire, was rebuilt and enlarged. New dressing rooms and a shower were added. Here Bowmer speaks with reporters and business people before a groundbreaking ceremony for the 1947 Elizabethan Theatre.

The 1947 stage was built from plans drawn by John Ashby Conway of the University of Washington. In his plans, he used all the dimensions mentioned in the contract for the construction of the 1599 Fortune Theatre. This provided a larger forestage and side stages, as well as backstage areas that had not previously existed.

THE FORTUNE THEATRE
MARCH 10
1 9 4 7

By 1949, thought was being given to further enlarging the Elizabethan Theatre. This drawing was published in the souvenir program with notes that there were plans to extend the balcony all the way around the shell, modifying the plan of the Fortune Theatre. Landscaped gardens with stylized borders and herbs and flowers mentioned in Shakespeare's plays would also be planted.

Despite the improvements, the theater facilities remained rudimentary. The plumbing backstage and the painting of the facade were not finished until 1948, and there was no roof over the backstage area. The only toilet was located in the adjacent YMCA building, and there was no privacy in the dressing rooms. Pictured are cast and crew members of the 1949 *Romeo and Juliet*.

The festival's board of directors rolled up its collective sleeves and built the benches pictured in the photograph. Angus Bowmer called the audience members "genuine Spartans," marveling at their ability to sit through three hours or more on hard benches and unstable folding chairs. There were no intermissions, and Bowmer did not cut scripts.

Actors Eddy Barron, Trubee Bell, and Suzanne LaMarre Hanson cool off in Ashland Creek for a 1948 publicity shoot. An OSF public relations writer at the time noted that "during festival days in Ashland, it's a common occurrence to see groups of the colorfully garbed Shakespearean players on the street." On the bridge, producing director Angus Bowmer is flanked by actor Franklin Reid (left) and costume designer Douglas Russell.

Garbed Shakespearean players gather for a publicity event at the Lithia Hotel in 1939 after the tour to San Francisco. An Associated Press article and photographs of this event appeared in *The Coast* magazine, a San Francisco publication. The article states, "Great men are often remembered in ways and places you would not expect, as Will Shakespeare's coming to the farmlands of southwestern Oregon testifies."

During the 1947 to 1948 academic year, Angus Bowmer took advantage of the GI Bill and studied at Stanford University. His decision was fortuitous for OSF, as he met individuals who would bring their expertise to Ashland, in turn encouraging others to come. Among those who arrived for the 1948 season were William Patton, later OSF's executive director, and Dr. Margery Bailey, who became director of the Institute of Renaissance Studies.

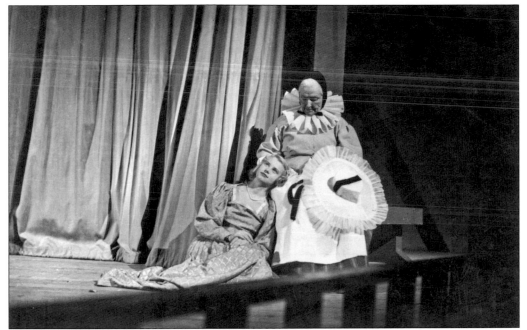

The 1949 production of *Romeo and Juliet* featured Dr. Margery Bailey (right) as the nurse in her first acting role at the festival, and Mary Jane Pitts as Juliet. OSF and the Portland Civic Theater had held auditions open to all Oregon high school students in order to find a Romeo and Juliet of an age indicated in the play. Pitts won the role of Juliet.

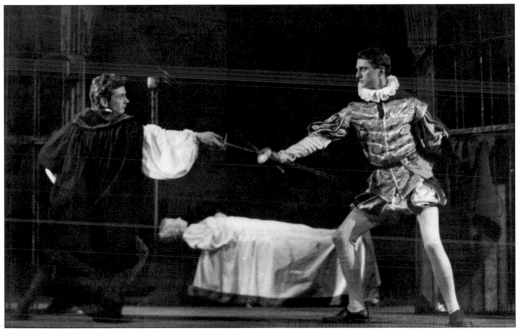

Bill Patton (right) worked as a lighting technician in the 1948 season, and in 1949 he returned from his studies at Stanford to resume technical work and to take on the role of Paris in *Romeo and Juliet*. Here he duels with Romeo, played by Ralph Burgess. Patton also played Henry Percy in *Richard II* that season.

In 1949, OSF added a fifth show to the repertory. In addition to *Romeo and Juliet* and *Richard II*, OSF staged *Othello*, *The Taming of the Shrew*, and *A Midsummer Night's Dream*. Here Angus Bowmer (right), who played Bottom, takes a break during a hot afternoon rehearsal to talk with Nicholas Gilroy, who played Lysander.

Publicity efforts by OSF and the Ashland Chamber of Commerce paid off when travel editors visited in 1950. Here they watch rehearsals of *The Comedy of Errors*. Pictured are, from left to right, (seated) Beverly Gray, *Calgary Herald*, and Polly Noyes, *San Francisco Chronicle*; (standing) Walter Humphrey, *Fort Worth Press*; John Cotton, president, OSF board; Angus Bowmer; Phil Stansbury, Ashland mayor; and William McGee, president, Ashland Chamber of Commerce.

Three

Stay Four Days, See Four Plays
1951–1969

The rebuilt, revitalized postwar festival encouraged playgoers to "Stay Four Days, See Four Plays, with Shakespeare Under the Stars." In 1953, OSF produced *Coriolanus*, the last of Shakespeare's tragedies, and *Henry VI, Part One*, the sixth of the history plays. With the production of *Troilus and Cressida* in 1958, OSF completed Shakespeare's canon for the first time. For Angus Bowmer, the greatest discovery was that even the weakest of the Bard's plays had "gut-gripping strength" for contemporary audiences. Attendance soared in the Elizabethan Theatre from 8,850 in 1950 to 59,619 in 1969, and it seemed that audiences agreed with Bowmer's assessment.

In 1951, OSF launched the first in a series of annual NBC coast-to-coast broadcasts from the festival stage under the direction of Andrew C. Love. The year 1952 marked the incorporation of the Tudor Guild, the festival's first volunteer organization, and the inaugural year of the Elizabethan Music Program. Musicians presented short musical programs of Renaissance music before three or four plays, and incidental music was integrated into the productions.

The following year, OSF hired its first full-time paid employee, general manager William Patton, and Richard Hay was appointed designer and technical director. Six years later in 1959, the new Elizabethan Theatre opened, designed by Hay and patterned on London's 1599 Fortune Theatre. To celebrate the opening, which also coincided with Oregon's centennial, Jerry Turner, in his directing debut at OSF, staged a state-commissioned prologue to *Twelfth Night*, titled *The Maske of the New World*, written by Carl Ritchie. The following year, OSF produced its first non-Shakespearean play, John Webster's *The Tragedy of the Duchess of Malfi*.

By 1960, OSF's Institute of Renaissance Studies, under the direction of Dr. Margery Bailey, was in its seventh year and offered courses, seminars, and lectures about the plays produced on stage each season.

By the mid-1960s, attendance was consistently at around 100 percent of capacity. In 1968 alone, 11,000 people were turned away at the box office. Thus, OSF jumped at the opportunity to produce a series of 18th-century ballad opera revivals at Ashland's Varsity Theatre from 1966 to 1969—all in anticipation of support for the idea of an indoor theater.

The City of Ashland and OSF collaborated to bring people to the community. Festival souvenir programs devoted numerous pages to area attractions, noting that if playgoers have "followed the suggestion of spending at least four days in Ashland to see the complete cycle of Shakespeare plays" they have an ideal chance to visit Lithia Park, the Twin Plunges, Crater Lake National Park, Diamond Lake, Oregon Caves, and historic Jacksonville.

Until 1959, auditions, casting calls, and technical and dress rehearsals were open to the public. As Angus Bowmer notes in his book, *As I remember, Adam,* many people in the valley not only saw the entire Shakespearean canon, but also the long process of bringing a play to the stage. Here directors of the 1951 productions, from left to right, Philip Hanson, James Sandoe, Richard Graham, and Bowmer, sit at an afternoon casting call.

Every company member did a bit of everything. Here they pitch in to repair, touch-up, and cleanup onstage, while another provides background music. The prompter's box was located at the front of the stage just over the rail. It contained the lighting and sound boards and a simple bench for the prompter, who frequently contended with bugs and spiders.

Richard Graham directed the 1951 production of *Twelfth Night*. Pictured are William Oyler (left), a Stanford graduate, as Orsino, and William G. Ball as Feste. Oyler, described by Angus Bowmer as "a very efficient and skillful technical director," would play many roles at OSF during the 1950s and early 1960s. Ball acted for two seasons at OSF, directed at numerous regional theaters in the 1950s and 1960s, and founded the American Conservatory Theater in San Francisco in 1967.

The first Vining Repertory was formed in the fall of 1951. Staged in the Lithia Theatre, the repertory produced four productions in November 1951, four the next spring, and four more that fall. The runs were increasingly successful, but in the midst of the 1952 fall season, a fire in the theater destroyed the stage, stock, treasury, and records. The college offered Churchill Hall for the remainder of the season.

In 1951, Bill Patton served as the lighting director at OSF and the Vining Repertory. He also assisted with public relations and publicity for the Vining Repertory and played a number of smaller roles in productions. He is pictured on the ladder with a local electrician to the left and Richard Graham and H. Paul Kliss on the right.

"Our beautiful little theater," as Angus Bowmer referred to the Lithia Theatre, was built by two brothers, one of whom was Prof. Irving Vining of the old Normal School. The theater opened in 1914 with the opera *Faust*. Both brothers were dead by 1951, so the festival decided to name the aspiring young troupe the Vining Repertory Company. (Courtesy of Southern Oregon Historical Society, negative 4237.)

In 1950, Bill Patton, pictured here, and Richard Hay sold fireworks in a rustic booth at the corner of Barnett Street and Highway 99 in Medford. They were assisted by others in the company, including Carol Eller and her husband, Bob Scothorn. The retail sales enabled Patton and Hay to pay for their summer in Ashland.

Two actors in their first seasons at OSF, George Peppard and Elizabeth Wattenberger pose for a publicity shot in Lithia Park. Peppard, who later gained fame as Audrey Hepburn's love interest in *Breakfast at Tiffany's*, acted in the 1951, 1953, and 1954 seasons. Angus Bowmer notes in his autobiography that however well Peppard performed in movies, he believed that Peppard's success in films deprived the theater of a great comic actor.

"Shakespeare can be fun" is the line in a publicity shot from the festival in 1953. Here Angus Bowmer, sitting center, poses with, from left to right (first row) actors William G. Ball, Joyce Womack, and Carolyn Sedey and director Allen Fletcher; (second row) actors Richard Weber, George Peppard, Howard Miller, Nicholas Probst, and Anne M. Lawder.

Actors in the 1953 season practice their fighting skills. Frank S. Pinnock gives Joyce Womack (right) a tip as she works with Carolyn Sedey. All three actors were cast in *Henry VI, Part One*—Pinnock as Somerset, Sedey as Joan la Pucelle, and Womack as a Fiend—and as the repertory required, each also played in two other productions. Pinnock was director of swordplay.

Jim and Eve Allen from Rogue River were ardent supporters of the festival. Beginning in 1947, they volunteered as gardeners, and each season they drove many miles from their ranch to tend the grounds. They dug flower beds, planted shrubs, pruned, mowed, and planted the ivy now covering the Chautauqua walls. Jim served for many years on the board of directors. Note the box office situated behind them.

John C. Cotton, president of the festival board of directors and owner of a local lumber mill, employed two actors, Richard Smith (shirtless) of West Lafayette, Indiana, and Jay Pender of Chicago, Illinois, both graduates of Purdue University. The actors were cast in the 1951 season and worked at the mill to earn money. Virginia Cotton also served as president of the board in 1957 and 1963.

Angus Bowmer always said that nothing given to the festival would go to waste. Lumber man John C. Cotton donated a huge piece of wood, and Martha Dawkins, an artist, Tudor Guild volunteer, and president of the guild in 1956, came up with the idea of a sign. Here she refreshes the paint.

In 1952, the local chapter of Beta Sigma Phi, a nonacademic organization for young women, decided to fund a scholarship each season for an actress in the festival. Beta Sigma Phi assumed management of the refreshment booth (contributions-only basis) on the festival grounds, and all money went to the scholarship fund. Scholarships from the festival and the Tudor Guild were also awarded to actors.

The information booth on the Ashland Plaza, operated by a Tudor Guild member, began operations in 1952. The early structure was rudimentary and described as "hardly more than four legs holding up a table." In 1959, a new structure was built, and volunteers provided motel and shopping information, as well as names of babysitters.

Richard Hay (right) and Edmund Chavez work in the scene shop in the basement of the Elizabethan Theatre in 1953. Hay was the technical director, and Chavez was his assistant. They were responsible for the design and construction of all scenic elements at the time. Hay was named art director in 1954. The souvenir program noted that the title was "an all-embracing term which requires him to do something of everything."

By 1954, the Tudor Guild was in its fifth year, though it was not incorporated until 1952. Founded through the efforts of Dr. Margery Bailey and Margaret Schuler of Medford, the original purpose of the guild was to raise money for a noninterest loan fund for festival actors. The annual Shakespeare Hey-Day, held in 1954 at the home of Mrs. Sprague Riegel (pictured here), was the principal fund-raising event.

Beginning in 1955, Hey-Day was held on the festival grounds. Activities included "penny pitch, darts, horse racing, Skittles, fish pond, bingo, wrestling, acrobatic tumbling, fencing and dancing." There was also a display of ancient musical instruments. Food included meat pies, cabbage slaw, Banbury tarts, saffron buns, gingerbread, ice cream cups, and more. Morris dancers and strolling minstrels provided additional entertainment.

Agnes David, a University of Texas teaching fellow and costume assistant, hems Joan Kugell's costume for the 1955 production of *All's Well that Ends Well*. Kugell played Helena. Costume designer Douglas Russell, whose designs are hanging on the wall, stated in the 1955 souvenir program that the costumes were based on "styles worn at the court of Henri III, modified and reinterpreted in asymmetrical lines and limited color contrasts."

Angus Bowmer continued to teach at Southern Oregon College (previously the Normal School and now Southern Oregon University) throughout his entire tenure as OSF's producing director. By 1955, when this photograph was taken, SOC offered a number of summer courses that were integrated with festival work. The festival also used space in the small buildings on the right to build costumes during the 1950s.

Angus Bowmer recalled that he had several years to observe Bill Patton grow into a knowledgeable and dedicated theater person. Patton, shown here operating the new lighting control board in the prompter's box in 1952, not only demonstrated a flair for lighting and publicity, but also for organizational detail. Bowmer recommended to the board of directors that Patton be appointed to the full-time role of general manager in the fall of 1953.

In 1954, from left to right, Eleanor Prosser, Joan C. Chavez, Marilyn C. Russell, and Anne Lawder Fletcher worked in the box office and performed on stage. The box office at the time was located in a small building next to the entrance to the Elizabethan Theatre. That year, the box office ticketed 18,476 people for 31 performances.

In 1956, the Feasting of the Tribe of Will (later called the Feast of Will) was first held in Lithia Park. After the feasting, pipers led the guests up to the theater. That year, Miss Oregon and Mark Hatfield, then in the state senate, attended the opening celebration and performance. Here they pose with a member of the Kilty Band and a copy of the souvenir program.

The 1957 production of *The Two Gentlemen of Verona* featured Angus Bowmer as Launce and Teddy "Seymour" as Crab, who are pictured studying lines. Also in this production, in his first season at the festival, was Nagle Jackson, who played Speed. Jackson played numerous roles at OSF into the 1960s and directed four productions. OSF produced two of his plays, *This Day and Age* and *Molière Plays Paris*.

Dr. Margery Bailey, director of the Institute of Renaissance Studies, is pictured here giving one of many public lectures and readings to further audiences' understanding of Shakespeare. Bowmer said that for the last 15 years of her life, "she shaped a unique education program which utilized our Elizabethan Theatre productions as a laboratory . . . so that reliable scholarship made a basis for an exciting theatricality inherent in the playwright's stage and script."

In 1951, Jennings Pierce of NBC radio, who had moved to KMED radio in Medford, arranged to produce a 30-minute broadcast of an abridged *King Lear* from the OSF stage. Andrew C. Love, pictured here with Angus Bowmer, produced the show and continued to create broadcasts for the next 25 years. Full-length recordings of season performances were done for the OSF archives and distributed to interested stations and schools.

Alfred S. V. Carpenter and his wife, Helene, were devoted supporters of the festival. For many years, the entire company was entertained each season at the Carpenter estate, Topsides, for a full day of eating, swimming, and relaxation. "Without the help of this truly gentle man," wrote Angus Bowmer, "the financing of the rebuilt Elizabethan Theatre in 1959 and the construction of the Bowmer Theatre in 1970 would have been impossible."

"Authentic in every detail," explains Angus Bowmer to Portlanders Doris Kyber and Don Ostensoe as he shows a replica of the 1947 theater, modeled on the 1599 Fortune Theatre, to Portland's KOIN-TV audiences in August 1956. Bowmer and Dr. Margery Bailey made several television and radio appearances during their one-day tour coordinated by Ostensoe and the First National Bank of Portland.

The 1957 souvenir program notes that the attractive facade of the 1947 theater hides the worsening situation of a weakened structure and congested space, which only a new festival theater could correct. Since 1947, as the seasons became longer and the technical requirements became more exact, additions to the theater became more haphazard until some areas had became quite dangerous.

Among the rough and unsafe areas were the dressing rooms located under the forestage of the Elizabethan Theatre. This photograph taken in 1957 shows the conditions. Because rainwater frequently leaked through the wooden floors overhead, plastic was draped from the ceiling to prevent moisture from dripping on makeup tables, costumes, and actors.

At the end of the 1958 season, the fire marshal deemed the Elizabethan Theatre a fire hazard and prohibited further performances. The old structure had to go and a fund-raising drive for a quarter of a million dollars for the new Elizabethan Theatre began. Angus Bowmer—hand on his head—along with Bill Patton watch as the theater comes down September 1, 1958, immediately at the end of the season.

The first step after completely tearing down the 1947 stage was to remove the old Chautauqua wall that had encircled the stage of the Chautauqua dome. Richard Hay's design for the 1959 theater incorporated all the stage dimensions mentioned in the 1599 Fortune Theatre contract, as well as making wise use of his many years of experience as a designer and staff member of OSF.

The old wall had to be demolished as the theater plans required a semi-octagonal footing not a circular one. Architect Jack A. Edson, based in Medford, and building contractor Frank Fairweather, also in business in the Rogue Valley, worked with Richard Hay on the project.

This view from Lithia Park of the construction of the new theater shows the basement area adjacent to the remaining Chautauqua wall. The steel supports are being put in place for what would be largely a wooden structure. Construction continued throughout the fall and winter, as the theater had to be ready by July 1959.

The new theater retained and enhanced the unusual atmosphere of the existing bowl. The seating remained the same (the concrete pad for seating had been poured in 1955); the rooftop of the concrete blockhouse (right foreground) behind the seating would be used by musicians and dancers, while the lighting, sound, and stage management booths were below. The rear of the bowl continued to provide space for gift and concession booths.

Construction of the theater took 11 months, and the paint was still wet when audiences filed in on July 28, 1959. Angus Bowmer wrote a public letter of appreciation to those who helped build the theater and gave of their time, money, and energy. "We thank you all," he wrote, "who built this monument . . . and generations of players and audiences yet unborn will be grateful that you were the builders."

In celebration of the 1959 opening of the Elizabethan Theatre and Oregon's centennial, the festival produced *The Maske of the New World*, written by Carl Ritchie, publicity director of OSF, and directed by Jerry Turner—his first directing assignment for OSF. Turner, who would succeed Bowmer as producing director, had acted in the 1957 productions of *Othello* and *King Lear* and the production of *The Merchant of Venice* in 1958.

On August 7, 1959, fire swept over the hills south of Ashland's Plaza. Nervous residents had packed their cars with their belongings, fearing the worst. At the festival, actors performed *Antony and Cleopatra* amid the sounds of exploding trees and crackling wood. But by the next morning, a firebreak and a change of wind saved the town. (Courtesy of Terry Skibby Collection.)

Performing on the evening of the fire were Margaret Vafiadis (left, later Margaret Rubin) as Charmian and Shirley Patton as Iras (with Edward Grover as Enobarbus). Actors remembered that the glow of the fire lit the audience as if it were daylight. Offstage, actors watched the fire from the back deck. Recalling that evening, Margaret Rubin said, "The fire definitely put on a better show than we did that night."

This late-1960s aerial shot of Ashland's watershed shows the path of the 1959 fire where the trees have begun to regrow. The shot was taken before the Angus Bowmer Theatre was built and after the Ashland Hotel was torn down in 1960. The YMCA building can be seen at the top of the Chautauqua walkway. (Courtesy of Terry Skibby Collection.)

In 1960, OSF produced its first non-Shakespearean play, John Webster's *The Tragedy of the Duchess of Malfi*. James Sandoe directed the play, and Ann Hackney played the Duchess of Malfi (pictured here). The cast and company were excited to be showcasing work by a contemporary of Shakespeare, and audiences responded positively.

Many well-known people traveled to the festival in the 1960s. Ginger Rogers, shown here with Angus Bowmer, came to the festival on a number of occasions. She had been the chairman of Southern California solicitations for the 1959 fund-raising drive. She often attended performances with her mother, coming from her ranch on the Rogue River. She was a good friend of OSF board member and historic preservationist Robertson Collins.

"This green plot shall be our stage." Surrounded by the mechanicals and in the role of Peter Quince, Angus Bowmer (center) may have found new significance in speaking these words during the 1961 performance of A Midsummer Night's Dream. He stood on the new Elizabethan Stage—in nearly the same place where some 30 years earlier, the idea of a festival had first captured his imagination.

A *Midsummer Night's Dream* was directed by B. Iden Payne, left, with actor Robert E. West. Payne had directed the festival's 1956 production of *Cymbeline*, but this was his first time on the new Elizabethan Stage. The presence of his mentor may have influenced Angus when he wrote his notes in that year's program: "The people who produce Shakespeare successfully in the 20th century are versed in scholarship as well as in theatre arts."

In 1960, director and producer Tyrone Guthrie (left) and his wife, Judith Bretherton, visited the festival, pictured with Bill and Shirley Patton. Guthrie had been the artistic director at the Stratford Festival in Canada, whose founder, Tom Patterson, had consulted with Angus Bowmer about ways to financially revive Stratford. Guthrie was traveling the West Coast seeking a place to build a theater. He opened the Guthrie Theater in Minneapolis in 1963.

The Vining Repertory Company was revived in 1961 at the Varsity Theatre through the sponsorship of Southern Oregon College. The festival produced four plays at the Varsity in November and December that year, a concert series in 1964, and from 1966 to 1969, a ballad opera series as well as the plays in the Elizabethan Theatre. Pictured is a volunteer hostess strolling through the Varsity lobby.

The Beggar's Opera was produced in 1966 and directed by Carl Ritchie. Angus Bowmer played Peachum and Pat Patton, who would work into the 1990s acting, stage managing, and directing at OSF, played Lockit. The musicals were hugely popular with audiences, and their appeal, Bowmer noted, pointed to the practicality of non-Shakespearean performances and the dire need for a theater in which to perform them.

In 1961, Charles Laughton (with actors Hugh Evans and Shirley Patton) told Angus Bowmer, "I have just seen the four best productions of Shakespeare that I have ever seen in my life. I wish Peter [Brook] could be here to see how Shakespeare should be done." Laughton begged to play King Lear after filming *Irma La Douce*. Bowmer agreed, but Laughton died in 1962 before he could fulfill the dream.

Hedda Hopper, a Hollywood columnist and personality and close friend of Ginger Rogers's mother, visited the festival and attended performances in September 1962. She attended the closing performances of *The Comedy of Errors* and *As You Like It* and was escorted by Robertson Collins, a Central Point businessman and festival board member.

From left to right, Green Show musicians Lucille Melinat, Kathleen Barnes, April Lewis, and Judy Bjorlie pose on the Elizabethan Stage for a 1964 publicity shot. The festival musicians and dancers worked long hours, rehearsing every morning (no dark Mondays), coming in for afternoon calls if they were performing in the evening's play, and preparing for and performing in the Green Show each evening.

After 1959, the Green Show musicians and dancers performed Renaissance numbers on the platform. As curtain time neared, the singers moved to the front of the theater to sing madrigals, a signal to move to one's seat. By the late 1980s, these short sets prior to the performance occurred less often as the Elizabethan costumes clashed with the style of the show on stage. The practice disappeared completely after 1997.

Jerry Turner directed the 1963 production of *Henry V*. Stacy Keach, in his second season at the festival, played the title role, and Elizabeth Huddle played the Queen of France. After his years at OSF, Keach would have a career in theater, television, and film. Huddle acted and directed in many regional theaters, and she became artistic director at the Intiman Theatre in Seattle in 1987 and the Portland Center Stage from 1994 to 2000.

Andrew C. Love holds a recording session on the Elizabethan Stage with actors in the 1964 production of *Henry VI, Part One*. The actors are, from left to right, Wes Carlson, Elisabeth Keller, Robert Page, Gail Chugg, Kirk Mee, and a young Patrick Page, who would later act at OSF, regional theaters, and Broadway. Love served as producer, director, and editor for recording the entire canon of Shakespeare as produced in Ashland.

The 1965 production of *Henry VI, Part Two* was directed by Edward S. Brubaker, who at that time was in his sixth season with the festival. King Henry was played by Laird Williamson, pictured on right with actors, from left to right, William Shephard, Richard Risso, and Peter Froehlich. Williamson has acted and directed at many regional theaters and continues to direct for OSF.

Duke Ellington and his orchestra played on the Elizabethan Stage in 1966 as part of a fund-raising celebration called *The Revels!!* The event brought in luminaries and 150 reporters. The two-and-one-half-hour concert included a brand new "Ad Lib on Nippon," since the orchestra had just visited Japan, and a host of standards such as "Don't Get Around Much Anymore."

Before the Angus Bowmer Theatre was built, the YMCA building was used for rehearsals, and the large house and Anne Hathaway's Cottage, a former restaurant, housed administrative offices. Behind the Elizabethan Theatre was the costume shop, built in the early 1960s, and the back deck was utilized for rehearsals during the day and as a green room during performances. With the construction of the Angus Bowmer Theatre, the three adjacent buildings were torn down and temporary offices were found downtown. The fund-raising drive for the new theater was led by Alfred S. V. Carpenter, and more than $1 million in contributions allowed the festival to move forward with construction plans. A federal Economic Development Administration (EDA) grant of $896,000—the first ever given to an arts-related project—helped ensure the project could continue. The federal grant also caused controversy in the community, as some residents felt the funds should go for other civic improvements rather than to building a theater.

In 1969, Richard Hay had returned for his 13th season on OSF's production staff. In addition to having designed the theater space of the 1959 Elizabethan Theatre, he was the theater design consultant for the Angus Bowmer Theatre, slated to open in March 1970. Richard worked with architects Kirk, Wallace, McKinley, AIA and Associates from Seattle and the contractor Robert D. Morrow, Inc., from Salem, Oregon.

The festival broke ground on December 18, 1968, and Bill Patton, pictured here, was a constant presence through the construction. Schedules were delayed when the city asked the festival to wait for the EDA grant to be processed. The EDA application also included remodeling of the administration building, a new box office, acquisition of the Black Swan building, conversion of a city block on Hargadine Street to a parking lot, and landscaping in nearby Lithia Park.

Work continued apace and pictured here are the large glue-laminated beams fanning outward from the stage, which support the audience area and extend above the lobby. Though there was controversy around the construction, ultimately Bill Patton and the festival received a huge outpouring of goodwill and support from the festival membership and the Rogue Valley community. More than $1 million was raised to match the EDA grant.

Angus Bowmer surveys the lobby area of the new indoor theater still under construction. Asked later how it felt to have a theater named after him, he replied, "I've always thought it more interesting to walk into one's monument than to lie under it. Not very many people have been able to do that."

Four

THE NEW REPERTORY
1970–1984

The 600-seat Angus Bowmer Theatre, designed by theater consultant Richard Hay and architect David McKinley, opened March 21, 1970, through the generous fund-raising efforts and contributions of the audience, community, and a federal matching grant. The theater opened with a performance of Tom Stoppard's *Rosencrantz and Guildenstern Are Dead*. The new indoor venue enabled OSF to expand its season into the spring and fall, offer matinee and evening shows, generate much-needed income, and accommodate more playgoers.

The following year Bowmer retired, and the challenge of guiding a Shakespeare company in search of a wider repertory fell to the newly appointed producing director Jerry Turner. OSF pursued the production of classics by Molière, Ibsen, Chekhov, and the like. Audiences loved the additions.

New logistical demands emerged with the expanded schedule, however, as everyone adapted to the complexities of the calendar. The shops were working on four productions for the spring opening and were then faced with building four more shows that would open in less than three months. Actors opened shows in the spring and started rehearsals for the summer productions a few days later. By 1976, the festival offered 277 performances of eight productions, and attendance was again exceeding 99 percent of capacity.

By the mid-1970s, there was talk of opening a third venue where more adventuresome contemporary pieces could be staged. In 1977, the Black Swan opened, and at the height of the season, three different theaters operated at the same time, each with its special demands and each with a different potential repertory. That same year, Bowmer and OSF received the Oregon Governor's Award for the Arts.

On May 26, 1979, Angus Bowmer died at the age of 75. That year, the festival produced 574 performances of 11 productions at 90 percent of capacity. Four years later, the festival won the Antoinette Perry (Tony) Award for outstanding achievement in regional theater and the National Governors' Association Award for distinguished service to the arts, the first ever awarded to a performing arts organization. Attendance topped 300,000 for the first time. Bowmer would have been proud.

The Angus Bowmer Theatre is pictured in winter 1970 before the bricks were laid. "The bricks" as they are still referred to today, formed a central plaza, linking the two theaters and the administrative building. The theater opened March 21 with *Stage II*, a six-week season through early May of four contemporary plays designed for students, parents, theater buffs, and vacationers.

The Angus Bowmer Theatre was a custom-designed theater conceived with both actor and audience in mind, placing them in one room without a proscenium framework. None of the 600 seats in the theater is more than 55 feet from the stage, and the seating is in continental fashion, with wide space between rows and no aisles. This 1975 photograph is shot from upstage of *The Winter's Tale* set.

Tom Stoppard's comedy, *Rosencrantz and Guildenstern Are Dead*, opened the Angus Bowmer Theatre in March 1970 with three other contemporary plays. The Stoppard play ran the entire season, while the others closed in early May. Two additional shows joined the repertory in the Bowmer Theatre in late May, and three Shakespearean productions ran on the outdoor stage. Pictured are Larry Carpenter (left) and Roger Kozol, with Loyd Williamson upstage.

This company photograph (with board members in front) was taken in 1970 on the set of *You Can't Take It With You*. The show was part of the *Stage II* season and was directed by Pat Patton, with scenic design by Richard Hay. The company photograph has become a tradition at OSF, though because the company now numbers more than 500, the photographs are taken on the Elizabethan Stage.

The "Stay Four Days, See Four Plays" banners of the 1960s were changed in the early 1970s with the opening of the Angus Bowmer Theatre. With the advent of *Stage II* and the expanded schedule, one could stay four days and see more than four plays. Matinee performances began in the 1970 season, with some student-only matinees. (Courtesy of Terry Skibby Collection.)

In late March 1971, the festival board of directors announced that Angus Bowmer (right) would assume new, broader duties as founder and development consultant. In mid-May 1971, a special board committee announced that Dr. Jerry Turner (left) had been unanimously selected to succeed Bowmer as producing director, effective June 15, 1971.

During a hot afternoon rehearsal in 1973, Laird Williamson, director of *Henry V*, talks with his cast. Powers Boothe, who played Henry V, looks on from the forestage. It was Williamson's fifth season at OSF. His cast included many who became festival favorites, including Mark Murphey, James Edmondson, Will Huddleston, Philip Davidson, and Denis Arndt.

A young woman in 1973 sells tarts before the performance in the Elizabethan Theatre. Maggie Skerry, who supported the work of the Tudor Guild in many ways, also provided the tart recipe. It is said that if the 14,496 tarts sold through the years were laid side by side, the line would extend from the Angus Bowmer Theatre to Ashland High School. The last tart was sold in 1997.

Mark Murphey is pictured as Kit Carson in the 1974 production of William Saroyan's Pulitzer Prize–winning play, *The Time of Your Life*, directed by Pat Patton. Asked years later why the production was so memorable, Patton explained that he had worked with a "magical ensemble." The cast included James Edmondson, Denis Arndt, Will Huddleston, Mary Turner, Warner Shook, and Shirley Patton.

In 1974, a devastating flood rushed through southern Oregon. Ashland found itself submerged in water as Ashland Creek flooded much of Lithia Park and the downtown. OSF company members, many of them residents of the community, pitched in to help with the cleanup, including actors James Edmondson (left) and Jeff Brooks, pictured here. As in 1974, after the 1997 flood, OSF company assisted with restoration work.

The Stanford University and OSF connection had been strong through the years, and in 1975, OSF personnel who were former faculty or students of Stanford gathered for a photograph. From left to right are (first row) Eric Booth Miller, Randi Douglas, and Angus Bowmer; (second row) John A. Caldwell, Richard Hay, Robert Loper, Peter Silbert, Shirley Patton, William Patton, and Jeannie Davidson.

Audrey Stanley directed the 1975 production of *The Winter's Tale*, becoming the first woman to direct a Shakespearean play at the festival. The cast featured James Edmondson, Peter Silbert, le Clanche du Rand, Randi Douglas, Mark Murphey, Shirley Patton, and JoAnn Johnson Patton. The first woman to direct at OSF was Margaret (Megs) Booker, who directed Ibsen's *Hedda Gabler* in 1974.

Students, pictured here in the Angus Bowmer Theatre, gave a standing ovation after a matinee performance of the 1975 production of *The Winter's Tale*. During *Stage II* spring performances, thousands of students attended the 13 student matinees. While in Ashland, students could also participate in actor-led workshops, post-play discussions, and take backstage tours. That same year more than 50 teachers attended a weeklong workshop on teaching dramatic literature.

Jerry Turner directed the 1975 production of Eugene O'Neill's *The Long Day's Journey into Night*. Pictured from left to right are actors Michael Kevin, William Hurt, and Jean Smart. Turner said of this play that O'Neill had finally faced his ghosts, lifting them "to a mythic plane where they will live and suffer forever as part of the permanent dramatic heritage of Western man."

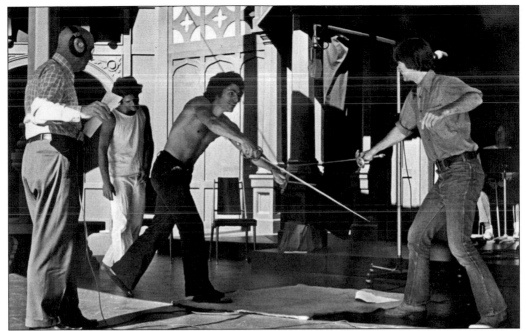

Producer Andrew C. Love, far left, records the clash of swords between Tybalt (left, Eric Booth Miller) and Romeo (Mark Murphey) for the complete audio recording of the 1975 production of *Romeo and Juliet*. Actor Judd Parkin, who played Benvolio, is in the back. This production was directed by James Edmondson, and Christine Healy played Juliet.

In 1975, company members and friends assembled at Bill and Shirley Patton's home to celebrate Andrew Love's 25th season of radio production for OSF. In his honor, Carl Ritchie wrote, "Many Brave Noises, a Salute to Andrew C. Love." The hour-long radio show featured reminiscences about radio from Love and associates. Pictured from left to right are Harry Skerry, unidentified, Al Reiss, Hazel and Andrew Love, and Angus Bowmer.

Marge McDowell (left, front), president of the Tudor Guild, stands with Gertrude Bowmer in 1975. That same year, the Tudor Guild endowed three festival scholarships perpetually by donating $15,000 to the endowment fund over 10 years, in addition to its annual $7,000 scholarship. The funds honored Gertrude Bowmer, Dr. Margery Bailey, and Margaret Schuler, cofounder with Dr. Bailey of the Tudor Guild.

Angus Bowmer's autobiography, *As I remember, Adam*, was published in 1975. A celebration was held at the Swedenburg House on the Southern Oregon State College campus, where the festival Exhibit Center was located. Pictured are Bowmer and Dorothy Pruitt reminiscing over the book. Jerry Turner wrote that Angus had certainly captured himself in print, but it had an unfinished quality because as the festival goes on, so does Angus.

In a 1976 publicity photograph for the Shakespeare Birthday Auction, actor Rex Rabold posed with a cheetah from Roseburg's Wildlife Safari. Rabold was offering his services as chef for a night to the highest bidder at the auction. The cheetah went home to Roseburg, and the winning bidder received a special behind-the-scenes walking safari with the director of zoology at Wildlife Safari.

Jerry Turner directed the 1976 production of *Henry VI, Part Two*. He was among the few who staged all three parts of *Henry VI*, directing part one in 1964 and part three in 1966. In 1976, Keith Grant played Suffolk and Jean Smart played Margaret. Grant advanced diversity casting at OSF, as he was the first African American to play a major Shakespearean role not designated as a character of color.

Pat Patton (left) was not only production manager, but he also worked as stage manager, actor, and director. He and Jerry Turner spent many afternoons and evenings in the seats of the Elizabethan Theatre. At the time of this photograph in 1976, Turner directed *Henry VI, Part Two*; Patton directed *King Lear* and also stage managed *Henry VI, Part Two*.

Pictured is the closing scene from the 1976 production of Henrik Ibsen's *Brand*, directed by Jerry Turner, which he also translated and adapted. Turner described it as "the least known great play in Western literature." Denis Arndt played the title role, with Christine Healy as Agnes and Virginia Bingham as Gerd. The memorable scenery of the avalanche was by Richard Hay, the costumes by Jeannie Davidson, and lighting by Thomas White.

On September 10, 1977, in the Angus Bowmer Theatre, the World Wizards of Wonder (pictured from left to right, Jerry L. Jones, Angus L. Bowmer, and Richard Hay) were featured in *Magic at Midnight*, a benefit for the festival scholarship fund for actors and technicians. Doors opened at 11:15 p.m., and attendees were asked to sponsor an actor's attendance by purchasing one ticket more than was needed.

Celebrating Shakespeare's birthday is an annual event at the festival, and in 1976, OSF company members celebrated the 412th birthday of William Shakespeare. Pictured lighting 412 candles are, from left to right, actors Dan Kremer, Brian Mulholland, Christine Healy, and Jerry Jones, and properties artisan Paul James Martin. Martin continues to work at OSF as senior properties master.

This photograph of Angus and Gertrude Bowmer was taken in 1976. Gertrude was born in Medford, Oregon, in 1903. She and Angus met when she attended a rehearsal of *Hamlet* in 1938, and they were married in December 1940 in Los Angeles. Through the years she was Angus's secretary and assistant, and friend and hostess to company members and dignitaries. He called her "my memory, my detail man, my secretary, my other self." She remained his primary assistant until his retirement as producing director in 1971. After Angus's death in May 1979, Gertrude served as honorary chair of the festival's 50th anniversary celebration in 1985 and of the campaign to raise funds for the Allen Pavilion in 1990. She also volunteered in the festival's Exhibit Center until 1993. She died on October 12, 1994.

In September 1976, the festival presented "Music, Dance and Verse of John Florio's England" in Carpenter Hall. The program was compiled and directed by Todd Barton, pictured here with a painting used as a backdrop for the concert, and choreographed by Judith Kennedy. Barton was music director and remains at the festival today as resident composer. Kennedy worked for 37 years at OSF as actor, dancer, costume assistant, and choreographer.

In addition to the allied volunteer organizations such as the Tudor Guild, Beta Sigma Phi, and Soroptimist International, who raise money for scholarships, volunteers still work in every department of the festival and on the board of directors. Here Belle Douglass, a longtime supporter of OSF and mother of Shirley Patton, works in the costume department in 1977. Ann Morrell, costume shop supervisor, is behind.

The building on the corner of Pioneer and Main Streets, across from the festival's administration building, went through many incarnations. For many years, it was a car dealership and then became Lyle's, a flooring business. Lyle's closed its doors in the mid-1960s, and the festival acquired the building in 1969. It served many purposes, including a rehearsal space and scene shop. The rehearsal space was used for Black Swan Projects, company-driven performances for company members. (Courtesy of Terry Skibby Collection.)

Richard Hay (right) with his assistant
William Bloodgood, in his first season
and later resident scenic designer at
OSF, stand with a model of Shelagh
Delaney's play A *Taste of Honey*. The
play opened the new Black Swan space
in 1977. Hay designed the theater
space, with assistance from technical
director Duncan McKenzie. The theater
seated 138 people and was created to
produce new and experimental work.

In 1977, properties assistant Paul James
Martin affixed the black swan appliqué
to the theater doors. Jerry Turner, in
describing why the name was chosen,
said that "the black swan was a beautiful
bird with an exotic color and a fierce
temper. It's a fitting emblem for what our
third stage should be." Lighting designer
Steven A. Maze had suggested the name.

With the final dabs of paint applied moments before the first patron entered the theater, the Black Swan was open. Pictured here, Jerry Turner addresses the audience at the opening ceremony in 1977. In the 1976 program, Turner wrote that the theater will "offer us the opportunity to explore work, both old and new, that cries for performance . . . The Black Swan will be a theater where we can stretch muscles."

Opening night in the Black Swan featured Shelagh Delaney's A Taste of Honey, directed by James Edmondson. The space was intimate and was described by theater designer Richard Hay in an interview as "an energy place, stripped for action." On stage are actors Margaret Rubin (left) and Cameron Dokey. Other actors in the show were Patrick DeSantis, Keith Grant, and Rex Rabold.

With the production of *Timon of Athens* in 1978, OSF completed the Shakespearean canon for a second time, and Richard Hay completed the canon as set designer for the first time. The Angus Bowmer Theatre provided an entirely new way of presenting the play. The first act was set in a contemporary Greek villa, and in the second act, the set revolved to reveal Timon's cave.

Since 1952, there has been a closing ceremony on the Elizabethan Stage after the final performance of the season. This photograph was taken at the 1978 ceremony, during which an actor speaks Prospero's words from Act IV, Scene I of *The Tempest*, beginning with "Our revels now are ended." Company members file into the aisles with candles, and then on completion of the speech, blow out the flames.

Festival musicians Richard Van Hessel, Patricia Maureen O'Scannell, David Marston, and Colleen Liggett perform in a 1982 OSF publicity photograph. The musicians and dancers' nightly "performance before the performance" presented songs and dances in a style true to the 16th century. Three different Green Shows, related in theme to the three outdoor plays, prepared audiences for the performance on stage that evening.

In the early 1980s, composer and music director Todd Barton (right) and sound engineer Douglas K. Faerber cocreated music and sound scores for numerous festival productions. Shown here in the sound booth of the Angus Bowmer Theatre, their collaborations included *Coriolanus*, *Troilus and Cressida*, *The Revenger's Tragedy*, and *Dracula*. Both Barton and Faerber continue to work at OSF.

Stuart Duckworth was part of the festival acting company from 1978 to 1982. His play *Dreamhouse* was first mounted as part of the 1981 series of Black Swan Projects. In 1983, OSF gave it a full production directed by Jerry Turner in the Black Swan. The set, pictured here, was by William Bloodgood. It was OSF's first world-premiere production.

In 1982, stitcher Vivienne Friedman (left) in her first season at OSF, works with first hand Deborah J. Barker on costumes for Noël Coward's *Blithe Spirit*, directed by Pat Patton. The costumes were designed by resident designer Jeannie Davidson. Actors in the production included JoAnn Johnson Patton, Richard Elmore, Shirley Patton, and Joan Stuart-Morris. Friedman continues to work in the costume shop as a cutter and draper.

Jerry Turner directed the 1982 production of *Julius Caesar*. "Purists will forgive us," he wrote, "for this unconventional approach to a well-known play." He used contemporary images to get closer to the spirit of the play, and the work took on new relevance as Anwar al-Sadat's assassination occurred shortly before rehearsals began. Joan Stuart-Morris, center, was a conspirator, the first time a woman played the role at OSF.

Dennis Bigelow (left) directed OSF's 1982 production of Lawrence and Lee's *Inherit the Wind*, which was based on the 1925 Scopes trial where William Jennings Bryan and Clarence Darrow argued the constitutionality of teaching evolution in schools. Phillip Davidson (right) played the Darrow character. Bigelow became artistic director at the Sacramento Theater Company, returned to OSF in 1988 to lead the Portland branch for several years, and then directed in other Portland theaters.

In 1982, company member Beth Bardossi drew the cartoon pictured here. During the summer months when tickets are in higher demand, people wait in line for the morning release of available seats. Bardossi humorously depicted the practice of lining up shoes in front of the box office window while individuals relaxed nearby or went for a cup of coffee. Bardossi continues to work at the festival in the publications office.

Jeannie Davidson (right) and Liz Col confer about costumes in the 1980s. Davidson joined the festival in 1964 and became resident costume designer in 1969, designing hundreds of productions for OSF. Col (now Liz Peck) was a stitcher in the costume shop for three years and then worked as Davidson's assistant for four years. They worked on four shows per year, often with two or three overlapping each other.

Actors Joe Vincent and Joan Stuart-Morris pose with the festival's 1983 Tony Award backstage after a performance of *Dracula*. They were among the hundreds who helped earn the award for distinguished achievement in regional theater. Richard L. Coe, critic emeritus for the *Washington Post*, and Al Reiss, local critic at Medford's *Mail Tribune*, were among the American Theatre Critics Association (ATCA) members who placed OSF in nomination for the Tony Award. When the Tony came home to OSF with Bill Patton, who received the award in New York City, the company celebrated with champagne. The award resides in the lobby of the Angus Bowmer Theatre.

Five

INVENTION AND CONTINUITY
1985–2010

While attendance, awards, and additions to the campus were easy markers of growth, it was always the work on stage that had to be the measure of OSF's success. Artistic director Jerry Turner saw OSF's mission as "finding a theatrical language appropriate to our times." The task of OSF, he said, was to make clear to current audiences the intent of the author's vision and the shared humanity in the themes of the plays.

Turner recognized that a playwright need not be dead to be worthy and suspected that in the coming years, OSF would pay more attention to living writers. Each succeeding artistic director has brought more new and diverse work to OSF's stages. Henry Woronicz and then Libby Appel greatly expanded commissions of new plays, translations, and adaptations. In 2008, Bill Rauch announced the largest commissioning project (37 plays) in the festival's history, *American Revolutions: the United States History Cycle.*

Shakespeare remained the standard, however, and the Elizabethan Stage was the primary platform for performance of his work. By 1990, it was apparent that the outdoor stage required a barrier to protect actors and audiences from light and noise. Neighbors, too, desired a buffer from the dramatic action. In 1992, the Allen Pavilion opened, providing a structural barrier, a new seating configuration, and improved acoustics and technical abilities.

At the same time, the Black Swan presented continuing challenges because of artistic limitations and obsolete facilities. In 2000, executive director Paul Nicholson and artistic director Libby Appel (appointed to their positions on the same day in 1995) presided over a groundbreaking ceremony for a new theater. Opened in 2002, the New Theatre provided flexible seating and increased capacity while maintaining the intimacy of the Black Swan.

In 2010, OSF celebrates its 75th anniversary. Bill Rauch, like Angus Bowmer, understands that theater must come from the people, and like all his predecessors, he believes that the stories presented onstage have the power to transform audiences and communities, and that OSF has the responsibility to tell those stories in the most powerful way possible.

OSF celebrated its 50th anniversary in 1985, and revived an early tradition of crowning a royal patron for the festival. Julia Powell (now Julia Woosnam) was enlisted to play Elizabeth, representing OSF at ceremonial occasions, including the Fourth of July parade. Powell worked in the administrative offices at the time, having also worked as a stitcher and dresser in the costume shop where she recently resumed work.

In 1985, the Green Show was in its 35th season since its inception in 1951. W. Bernard Windt became the music director in 1952, and Todd Barton took over in 1972. Judy Kennedy choreographed the dances for 26 years. The nine dancers in 1985 were, from left to right, Shane Henry, Kristin Patton, Tom Scales, Rena Zentner, Martin Prelle-Tworek, Sonja Wold, James Giancarlo, Adair Lamborn, and Juan A. Dominguez.

In 1985, Versatile Video recorded the reminiscences of William Cottrell, seated left, actor and director in the 1930s and 1940, with Jerry Turner. Cottrell was from Medford and taught at the Cornish School of the Arts in Seattle. He worked with Angus and Lois Bowmer and Robert Stedman to begin the festival. The interview was part of a documentary, *The Dream Begins*, chronicling the festival's years from 1935 to 1947.

The festival produced Steve Metcalfe's *Strange Snow* in the Black Swan during the 1985 and 1986 seasons. The play featured Jeanne Paulsen as Martha, sister of David, who was played by Richard Elmore (pictured here), and Bill Geisslinger, who played Megs. Both Elmore and Geisslinger and the characters they played were Vietnam veterans.

In 1986, the festival was among the recipients of the President's Volunteer Action Award. Office manager Shelly Lara (left, now Shelly Hensarling) and volunteer Maxine Hunnell, who had assisted Lois Bowmer with costumes in the 1930s and continued to volunteer in the Exhibit Center, traveled to Washington, D.C., to receive the award. The award was established in 1982 by Pres. Ronald Reagan to recognize, promote, and reward volunteerism.

In 1987, actor and director James Edmondson proposed that OSF should hold a fund-raiser for HIV/AIDS charitable organizations. Too many people were being lost to the disease, and OSF needed to help. Jerry Turner named the event the Daedalus Project after the story of Daedalus from Greek mythology. Pictured in the foreground are, from left to right, actors Demetra Pittman, Colleen Stanton, Ann Bass, and Dawn Lisell rehearsing for the 1988 event.

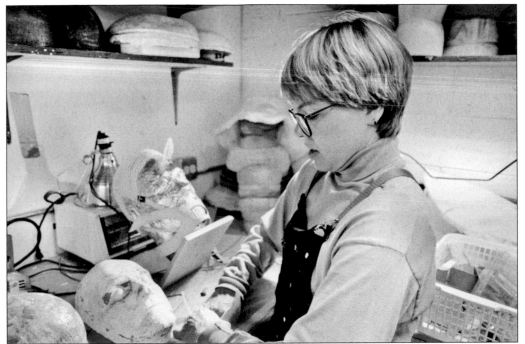

In 1987, costume props artisan Wendy J. Fountain worked on masks and fairy caps for *A Midsummer Night's Dream*. This was Fountain's first season at the festival, and at the time, the costume shop was located in the lower level of the Elizabethan Theatre. The costume shop moved into its current location in the Pioneer Building on Main Street in 1997, and Fountain continues her work in costume props.

William A. Henry III, standing, theater critic for *Time* magazine, was the featured speaker at the 1987 season opening luncheon held at the Oregon Cabaret Theatre. Henry was a Pulitzer Prize–winning journalist who covered the festival in 1986. Seated at the table from left to right are Margaret Rubin, Gertrude Bowmer, Jerry Turner, Mary Turner, William Henry's wife, and Bill Patton.

OSF's 1987 production of *Richard II* featured Rex Rabold as Richard. Stage manager for the production, Kimberley Jean Barry, recalled that for each performance Rabold tilted the mirror, capturing light on his face as he spoke, "Hath Sorrow struck so many blows upon this face of mine, and made no deeper wounds? A brittle glory shineth in this face, as brittle as the glory is the face."

The 1988 production of Luigi Pirandello's *Enrico IV* (*The Emperor*) ranks high among the memorable festival productions. Libby Appel, in her first season at OSF, directed, and the cast featured Rex Rabold as Henry IV and Linda Alper as Donna Matilde Spina, pictured here. Scenic design was by William Bloodgood, costumes by Jeannie Davidson, lighting by Robert Peterson, and music by Todd Barton.

The City of Portland first approached OSF about joining the Portland arts scene in the late 1970s, when Bill Patton and Richard Hay were invited to serve on a committee to find an existing building that would be suitable to house theaters as part of the Portland Center for the Performing Arts. The search determined that no appropriate facility existed, and the decision was made to build a new center. In 1986, OSF was again approached about producing in the new Portland Center for the Performing Arts. On November 17, 1988, OSF Portland was launched under the artistic leadership of Dennis Bigelow. Performances were held in the Intermediate Theatre, and audiences were offered a season subscription of five plays.

The opening production at OSF Portland was Shaw's *Heartbreak House*, which featured Sandy McCallum as Captain Shotover and Robynn Rodriguez as Ellie Dunn, both in their first season with OSF. The production was directed by Jerry Turner, the set was by William Bloodgood, costumes by Deborah M. Dryden, and lighting by James Sale.

Shakespeare's *Pericles Prince of Tyre* was also produced at OSF Portland in the 1988–1989 season. Pictured, from left to right, are Kathleen Turco-Lyon as Thaisa, J. P. Phillips as Simonides, and Derrick Lee Weeden as Pericles. Codirected by Jerry Turner and Dennis Bigelow, the production transferred to OSF's Angus Bowmer Theatre in April 1989. It was the first of four productions that transferred to or from Ashland during OSF Portland's six-season run.

100

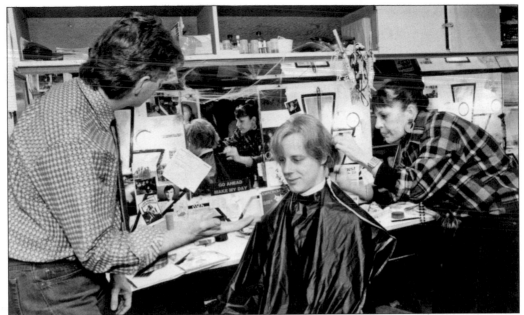

In this 1988 photograph, costume designer Michael Olich (left) and wig builder Ranny Beyer finesse a hand-tied toupee for actor Remi Sandri, who played Mercutio in *Romeo and Juliet*. The wig and hair artisans interpret the designer's renderings to create unique styles for each actor that work with their character as well the actor's skin tones and facial features. Beyer joined OSF in 1971 and is the principal wig builder.

Under the guidance of OSF board member Ancil Payne and with the support of Boeing Corporation, the festival hosted the annual Seattle fly-in for several years in the late 1980s. Payne was president and chief executive officer of the Seattle-based King Broadcasting Company, and he gathered many corporate executives for the excursions. Participants had dinner on the plane, were transported from Medford for a play on the Elizabethan Stage, and then returned home that evening.

Receptionist Kathy Claussen, pictured here at her desk in 1990, continues to be responsible for answering thousands of questions, phone calls, and requests during the course of a busy season. Through her 30 years with the festival, her desk has moved many times, as the administrative building has undergone its many changes.

Archivist Kathleen F. Leary, pictured in 1991 in the vault of the historic bank building, the only archives space at the time, views a photograph of Randi Douglas, who played Joan la Pucelle in the 1975 production of *Henry VI, Part One*. As part of her duty to illuminate the historical records of OSF, she displays images from past productions of the plays currently on stage in festival theater galleries.

In the 1990–1991 season, OSF Portland experimented with rotating repertory (standard practice in Ashland, but not in Portland) and produced both Timberlake Wertenbaker's *Our Country's Good* and George Farquhar's *The Recruiting Officer*, directed by Dennis Bigelow. A company of 10 actors performed 43 roles, often on the same day, and demonstrated to audiences the range of their skills in the two highly theatrical productions. Demetra Pittman, in her sixth season with OSF, played Melinda (above, right) and Leigh Clark played Silvia (above, left) in *The Recruiting Officer*. Pittman also played Liz Morden, a convict (at right), in *Our Country's Good*. Artistic director Jerry Turner noted, "What we are trying to do collectively as a company is larger than the sum of the parts. It's the theme of *Our Country's Good*—the convicts, the dregs of humanity, can be ennobled by acting something beyond themselves."

In 1990, master carpenter Bruce Jennings was among those building the plays' physical environments. In this photograph, he was working on the Shaughnessy apartment, c. 1965, for John Guare's *The House of Blue Leaves*, directed by Sandy McCallum. Jennings began working at the festival in 1979 and is a construction supervisor at OSF.

Since the early 1990s, OSF has worked to make performances and offstage events accessible to all patrons. The performance of *The Merchant of Venice* on March 26, 1991, was sign-interpreted by Jana Owen (left) and Jennifer Reese. On stage, Robert Lisell-Frank (right, now Robert Vincent Frank) played Launcelot Gobbo and Karin Johnson was Jessica, Shylock's daughter. OSF continues to offer sign-interpreted and open-captioned performances and audio description.

By the late 1980s, it became increasingly clear that audiences in the Elizabethan Theatre could not hear the actors because of ever-increasing ambient noise. In 1989, festival leaders resolved to build an enclosure for the Elizabethan Stage that would contain the actors' voices within the theater and keep street noises outside. In addition, it was decided to incorporate other changes—to extend the stage, add vomitoria, improve sightlines, and expand the lighting. Pictured are the grounds of the festival before the pavilion was built, and the pavilion in the midst of construction. The pavilion was designed by Treffinger, Walz, and MacLeod in consultation with Richard Hay and S. Leonard Auerbach and Associates.

Ground was broken for the pavilion on September 30, 1991. Within minutes of the ceremony, a huge grapple toppled a portion of the Chautauqua wall (later rebuilt) and for eight months, a well-directed construction schedule was followed. In the photographs, the beams for the new balcony are being placed, and the steel skeleton of the pavilion reveals the walkways to access the new lighting capabilities. With the addition of the balcony, the seating configuration changed, but the seating capacity of 1,198 did not. The new structure was complete for the opening of the 1992 summer season. The Allen Pavilion was named in honor of the Allen Foundation for the Arts, the largest contributor to the project.

With the construction of the Allen Pavilion, the blockhouse that had served as a platform for Green Show performances was gone. For a short time, musicians played on a small raised stage outside the pavilion, but within the walls of the theater. Crowding and space issues made this an inadequate solution. In 1994, a dance deck was built on the OSF bricks, improving the performance space and audience viewing.

Among the highlights of the Daedalus Project was a hat parade during the intermission of the evening's variety show. Participants from various departments created hats representative of some of the day-to-day activities of their department, and audience members would vote for their favorite hats with donations of hard cash. In 1991, general manager Paul Nicholson wore a millinery confection of administrative tidbits.

Costume renderings, such as the one above by designer Jeannie Davidson, are translated into patterns by cutters in the costume shop, from which the costume can then be cut and sewn, making the original concept into a three-dimensional wearable reality.

Henry Woronicz was appointed artistic director in 1991, his eighth season as actor and director at OSF. He hoped to deepen the work at OSF, and his goals included greater reliance on the unadorned facade and power of Shakespeare's words in the Elizabethan Stage and pared down scenic elements in the Black Swan. That year, Woronicz played Petruchio in *The Taming of the Shrew*, pictured here with Sheryl Taub as Katherine.

In 1993, the festival produced August Wilson's *Joe Turner's Come and Gone*, the first Wilson play staged in Ashland and chronologically the first in Wilson's series of history plays (at the time, before *Gem of the Ocean* was written). Directed by Clinton Turner Davis, the cast included, from left to right, LeWan Alexander, J. P. Phillips, and Derrick Lee Weeden. Since 1993, OSF has produced six of Wilson's plays.

Costume design assistant (and expectant mother) Lauren Toppo assists actor Aldo Billingslea with his costume during a fitting for *Joe Turner's Come and Gone*, as costume designer Candace Cain looks on. Toppo began her career at OSF in 1989 and continues to work in costume props, creating hats, masks, armor, jewelry, shoes, boots, and the many accessories that further enhance the costumes.

The Two Noble Kinsmen, by William Shakespeare and John Fletcher, is one of the less-produced Shakespeare plays, and controversy over its authorship has often prompted its exclusion from many collections of Shakespeare's work. OSF produced the play in 1994 on the Elizabethan Stage. Directed by Nagle Jackson, the cast included Robin Goodrin Nordli (left) and Eileen DeSandre. It was the first season in Ashland for both actors.

OSF's School Visit Program was created in 1973 by Angus Bowmer and made possible through NEA funding. Since 1973, actor-teacher teams of two or three have traveled throughout the West Coast, reaching as many as 140,000 students, a large percentage of whom will travel to OSF to see performances. In 1996, actor-teachers Derrick Lee Weeden and Cindy Basco traveled to Northern California. Weeden is pictured here with elementary students in Davis, California.

Theater has always been about the art of collaboration, and since OSF's beginnings, at the first rehearsal of plays, everyone involved in the production and many in the company assembled to hear the director and others introduce the play and talk about their roles in its production. In 1996, OSF produced Nagle Jackson's *Molière Plays Paris*, and pictured here are scenic designer Michael Ganio (left), who discussed the set he created, and Scott Kaiser, voice and text director on the play, who talked about his role. More than 80 people were listed in the playbill as having a hand in putting this play on stage. These included scene shop artisans who built the set, pictured here under construction. In the course of six weeks, four carpenters, two scenic painters, and two welders spent 1,400 hours working on the set.

Libby Appel was appointed artistic director in 1995, but the first season to bear her stamp was the 1997 season. She chose to direct *King Lear*, which featured James Edmondson (right) as King Lear and Demetra Pittman as the Fool. Appel's production emphasized family relationships, aging, and loss of power. To further reinforce this theme, she placed *Death of a Salesman*, which treats similar material in modern terms, on the same playbill.

Bow Seltzer (left) and Arnold Kohnert change the display at the OSF Exhibit Center after the 1997 season, incorporating set pieces from *Death of a Salesman* and *The Two Gentlemen of Verona*. The center opened in 1975 at the Swedenberg House on the college campus, then moved to Main and Pioneer Streets in 1980. It closed in 2000 and was remodeled for a welcome center and space for educational activities.

Performing in repertory not only allows for audiences to see actors play different roles from matinee to evening performance, but also to experience contrasting theatrical milieus created by designers, who also have the opportunity to stretch their artistic muscles in repertory. In 1997, audience members might walk into the Angus Bowmer Theatre at a matinee and see the highly presentational and art deco set of *Rough Crossing*, above, designed by Richard Hay, and return that evening to see the full-stage minimalist setting of *Death of a Salesman*, below, by Ming Cho Lee. The contrast is stunning and made possible by a stage operations crew that does a highly choreographed and exacting set change, ensuring that the exchange occurs in time for light check, dance and fight call, and the house is ready for an audience by half-hour.

Artistic director Libby Appel and executive director Paul Nicholson addressed the company at the 1998 company call in the Angus Bowmer Theatre. The annual assembly provides the opportunity for company members to introduce themselves and the leadership to share hopes and expectations. That season, in addition to six classic and contemporary productions, OSF produced five Shakespeare plays.

In 1998, OSF's production of Lorraine Hansberry's *Les Blancs* was videotaped for the New York Public Library for the Performing Arts at Lincoln Center's Theater on Film and Tape Archives (TOFT). Pictured is a TOFT representative, front, with OSF production stage manager Kimberley Jean Barry in the lobby of the Angus Bowmer Theatre during the recording session. TOFT holds six OSF production videos, dating from 1985.

Music has been an integral part of OSF productions from the beginning. Over the years, the use of music in plays has varied based on the style and direction of each unique production. In 1998, Penny Metropulos, director of *A Midsummer Night's Dream*, worked with the jazz trio Oregon to compose music. From left to right are Ralph Towner at keyboard, Glen Moore on bass, and Paul McCandless on woodwinds.

OSF's Diversity Council formed in 1995 through the collaborative efforts of actor LeWan Alexander, artistic director Henry Woronicz, associate artistic director Fontaine Syer, then general manager Paul Nicholson, and others. Diversity efforts expanded under Libby Appel's leadership, and associate artistic director Timothy Bond (second from right) managed the program. OSF hired Joseph Quinones (front right) as diversity consultant. Here they talk with members of the costume department.

The Tudor Guild Gift Shop had many locations, but in December 1997, the shop moved from the lower level of the administrative building to its current quarters across from the Angus Bowmer Theatre. That year, when enormous resources were required to make the move, the guild was still able to contribute a gift of $175,000 to the festival.

Lillian Garrett-Groag's *The Magic Fire*, directed by Libby Appel, premiered at OSF in 1997 and then toured to the Eisenhower Theater stage at the John F. Kennedy Center for the Performing Arts in Washington, D.C., in November 1998. The play was the first OSF production to be staged at the Kennedy Center. Pictured from left to right are actors Dee Maaske, Demetra Pittman, Kenneth Albers, Judith-Marie Bergan, and Catherine E. Coulson.

The Green Show transformed in 1998 when artistic director Libby Appel invited Indiana-based Dance Kaleidoscope to join OSF as the resident dance company and work with the Terra Nova Consort, OSF's resident musical ensemble for 10 years (though not under the same name). Pictured from left to right are musicians David Rogers, Nancy C. Elliott, Robert Dubow, Sue Carney, Bryce Peltier, and Nicholas Tennant. The gravity-defying dancer is Ricardo Melendez.

In 1999, company members Linda Alper, Douglas Langworthy, and Penny Metropulos adapted Alexandre Dumas's *The Three Musketeers* for the Elizabethan Stage. The production featured lush period costumes by resident designer Deborah M. Dryden, adventure, intrigue, and many swordfights. In a fight rehearsal, assistant fight choreographer U. Jonathan Toppo (left), who also played Aramis, lunges at Christopher DuVal, who played a Cardinal's Guard.

John Sipes demonstrated to the board of directors in 1999 some of the techniques he used in working with actors on *The Three Musketeers*, for which he was associate director and fight choreographer. Sipes was the festival's resident fight and movement director for many years, not only working with actors to choreograph fights but also to reach the goal of the appearance of effortless movement in finding the outlook and physical awareness of their characters.

From left to right, scenic artists Cynthia Schurter, Patrick Bonney, and Konnie May relax on the 1999 set of Maurine Watkins's *Chicago*. The scenic design by William Bloodgood featured a back wall and flooring that looked like a 1920s newspaper. The artists made six large silk screen stencils and cut lines from newspaper articles, which they fit in justified columns. After stenciling their clothes, they posed for the photograph.

118

Robin Goodrn Nordli played the Chorus in the 2000 production of *Henry V*, directed by Libby Appel. Nordli, a veteran with OSF, was the first woman to play the role at the festival. The Chorus sets the stage for Shakespeare's highly patriotic story about Henry V and his battle against the French with the words: "Oh for a muse of fire that would ascend / The brightest heaven of invention!"

Months before a play is staged, the director and designers hold numerous meetings to discuss how the world of the play will be presented. Pictured is the 2001 design team of Regina Taylor's *Oo-Bla-Dee*, from left to right, projections designer Sage Marie Carter, costume designer Lydia Tanji, scenic designer Richard Hay, music and sound designer Todd Barton, and director Timothy Bond.

In 2001, OSF staged Pedro Calderón de la Barca's Spanish classic, *Life Is a Dream*, directed and adapted by Laird Williamson. Vilma Silva (left) played Rosaura, pictured with a horse created by the properties staff and brought to life by actors James J. Peck and Gerson Dacanay. The horse was one of thousands of properties created by artisans that, with an actor's ability, can lure audiences into the illusion and play's reality.

In October 2001, prior to the matinee performance of Nilo Cruz's *Two Sisters and a Piano* in the Black Swan, executive director Paul Nicholson, center, welcomed Richard Anderson of Ashland, the 10-millionth ticket holder to walk through the festival doors. The festival welcomed its 1-millionth visitor in 1971, and its 20-millionth visitor is due in approximately 2015.

Throughout the 1990s, OSF leadership had discussed internally the need for a new theater space to replace the obsolete Black Swan. In early 1999, the festival publicly announced its intention to create a new theater. Initially, OSF considered moving Carpenter Hall to a different location in Ashland so that it might be used by the community, but an outcry from some residents caused OSF to reconsider. The New Theatre's footprint was changed, and Carpenter Hall remains on the festival campus. The public phase of OSF's $23 million capital campaign (which included $10 million for the endowment fund) was announced in June 2000, and at that time, through the generous gifts of the Allen Foundation for the Arts and many others, 71 percent of the funds had already been raised.

Executive director Paul Nicholson and artistic director Libby Appel, pictured together during construction, worked to ensure that communication stayed open with the various specialists and stakeholders in this huge project. The New Theatre building design was by Thomas Hacker and Associates of Portland, Oregon, the theater space design by Richard Hay, and acoustical engineering by Dohn and Associates of Morro Bay, California. The contractor was Emerick Construction of Portland.

The state-of-the-art theater plans were unique, as they included the ability to change the configuration of audience seating from three-quarter thrust, to avenue, to arena, accommodating 240–360 people and creating new artistic choices and audience experiences. The New Theatre received the 2005 Chicago Athenaeum American Architecture Award, the 2002 AIA Portland Chapter Craftsmanship Award for Excellence in Concrete, and was selected for exhibit at the 2007 Prague Quadrennial Exhibition.

The grand opening of the New Theater was March 1, 2002, with a performance of *Macbeth* directed by Libby Appel. Set design was by Richard Hay, who has designed hundreds of sets for the Elizabethan, Angus Bowmer, and Black Swan Theatres; with the opening of the New Theatre, he had another playground. *Macbeth* was staged in the round, and at the center was a simple disk with a pool of blood. The small space and minimal scenery emphasized the director's desire to focus on Macbeth's psychology. In comparison, Hay's design for David Lindsey Abaire's 2007 production of *Rabbit Hole* in three-quarter thrust configuration was a realistic setting where actors and audiences shared the intimate space of the living room of a family in crisis.

OSF's backstage tours began in 1958 and have always been important to the enhancement of a playgoer's experience. The tour takes patrons into each theater, the Angus Bowmer Theater's green room, and backstage in the Elizabethan. Guides are generally actors, artisans, or technicians. Kimberley Jean Barry schedules and educates tour guides. Pictured is actor Nicol Foster in 2002, who explains to a group the complexities of a run sheet.

Time magazine rated the OSF and Berkeley Repertory Theatre production of David Edgar's *Continental Divide: Mothers Against* and *Daughters of the Revolution*, directed by Tony Taccone, the number one best theater experience for 2003. The plays premiered at OSF, ran at Berkeley Repertory Theater, moved to England's Birmingham Repertory Theatre and London's Barbican Theatre, and returned to La Jolla Playhouse. Among the cast were, from left to right, Robynn Rodriguez, Christine Williams, and Bill Geisslinger.

In 2004, Libby Appel and Scott Kaiser adapted and codirected the three parts of Shakespeare's *Henry VI*, presenting them as two plays in two different venues with the same cast. *Henry VI, Part One: Talbot and Joan* played in the New Theatre; *Henry VI, Parts Two and Three: Henry and Margaret* played on the Elizabethan Stage. Pictured are Tyler Layton (right) as Joan la Pucelle and Laura Morache as the Vision.

Since the 1959 Elizabethan Stage was built, it has been the tradition that a member of the stage operations crew raises the OSF flag five minutes before the evening's performance. Pictured is Chris Chalk, greeting the audience before a 2005 performance. The flag was designed by Richard Hay and features Shakespeare's coat of arms (reversed) and the crest, a falcon holding a spear, and ash leaves, signifying Ashland.

In 2007, actor Rex Young talked with audiences in a postshow discussion in the Elizabethan Theatre. Young went to high school in Ashland and began his career with OSF in 1983 selling tarts. Karl Backus, a former actor at OSF, has said of Rex, "He's the poster boy for what OSF is all about—exposure to the theater at a young age, creating a passion that informs a life."

Festival company members have appeared in Ashland's Fourth of July parade in many different disguises. In the 1970s and 1980s, festival company members marched as the Talent Tomato Festival and Precision Marching Band. Casual, spontaneous, and fun, the band's antics were a hit. In 2008, some company members resurrected the tomatoes and are shown here attempting precise marching order.

Artistic director Bill Rauch (left) and executive director Paul Nicholson applaud the 16 current and former company members who worked 30 or more years at OSF. In 2005, the festival began to recognize the many years that staff have given to OSF. There are 78 people who have worked more than 20 years at OSF, and 221 that have worked more than 10 years.

In 2009, OSF produced the world-premiere production of *Equivocation* by Bill Cain. Directed by artistic director Bill Rauch in the Angus Bowmer Theatre, the play is about Shakespeare (played by actor Anthony Heald, pictured here), his acting company, their cooperative venture, and the quest for the truth. The play was the first OSF production to feature Shakespeare as a character.

ACROSS AMERICA, PEOPLE ARE DISCOVERING SOMETHING WONDERFUL. *THEIR HERITAGE.*

Arcadia Publishing is the leading local history publisher in the United States. With more than 5,000 titles in print and hundreds of new titles released every year, Arcadia has extensive specialized experience chronicling the history of communities and celebrating America's hidden stories, bringing to life the people, places, and events from the past. To discover the history of other communities across the nation, please visit:

www.arcadiapublishing.com

Customized search tools allow you to find regional history books about the town where you grew up, the cities where your friends and family live, the town where your parents met, or even that retirement spot you've been dreaming about.